First Workshop on Natural Language Processing for Human Resources (NLP4HR 2024)

St. Julian's, Malta
22 March 2024

ISBN: 978-1-7138-9457-5

Printed from e-media with permission by:

Curran Associates, Inc.
57 Morehouse Lane
Red Hook, NY 12571

Some format issues inherent in the e-media version may also appear in this print version.

Printed with permission by Curran Associates, Inc. (2025)

Association for Computational Linguistics
209 N. Eighth Street
Stroudsburg, Pennsylvania 18360

Phone: 1-570-476-8006
Fax: 1-570-476-0860

acl@aclweb.org

Additional copies of this publication are available from:

Curran Associates, Inc.
57 Morehouse Lane
Red Hook, NY 12571 USA
Phone: 845-758-0400
Fax: 845-758-2633
Email: curran@proceedings.com
Web: www.proceedings.com

NLP4HR 2024

The First Workshop on Natural Language Processing for Human Resources (NLP4HR 2024)

Proceedings of the Workshop

March 22, 2024

The NLP4HR organizers gratefully acknowledge the support from the following sponsors.

Megagon Labs

Association for Computational Linguistics (ACL)
209 N. Eighth Street
Stroudsburg, PA 18360
USA
Tel: +1-570-476-8006
Fax: +1-570-476-0860
acl@aclweb.org

Introduction

Welcome to the first Workshop on Natural Language Processing for Human Resources!

The field of human resources (HR) encompasses a wide range of tasks where the application of natural language processing (NLP) holds significant promise. Applications such as talent acquisition, career development guidance, performance management, and ongoing education and training involve a substantial amount of unstructured, semi-structured, and structured data. NLP can offer (semi-)automated solutions to address the challenges associated with these tasks. At the same time, the integration of AI in HR applications also presents certain risks and concerns, such as fairness, privacy, reproducibility, controllability, and transparency. There is an enormous opportunity to leverage advanced NLP techniques to address these challenges. These areas not only intersect with established NLP tasks but also overlap with fields like data mining and management, which have inspired workshops across various communities. These workshops include the Workshop on Recommender Systems for Human Resources, the International Workshop on Talent and Management Computing, and the International Workshop AI for Human Resources and Public Employment Services. The NLP4HR workshop specifically aims to bring together NLP researchers and practitioners to advance innovative solutions for HR challenges.

For this inaugural edition of the NLP4HR workshop, we received 11 original research submissions. Thanks to the diligent efforts of our Program Committee members, we curated a collection of 6 original research contributions (an acceptance rate of 55%). Furthermore, we will feature one paper from the EACL Findings during the workshop. We believe that these papers will inspire the research community and lay a solid foundation for ongoing and future endeavors in this area.

In addition to the presentation of research papers, the workshop will feature invited talks and a panel discussion, providing a platform for participants to exchange ideas and experiences through open discussions. We are pleased to have the following invited speakers: Trey Causey (Indeed), David Graus (Randstad), Marko Grobelnik (Jozef Stefan Institute, OECD, European Union Commission), and Barbara Plank (Ludwig-Maximilians-Universität München, IT University of Copenhagen). They will cover a range of critical topics associated with NLP applications in the HR domain. The panel, titled "HR in the Era of Large Pre-trained Models: Sorting out *the Good, the Bad, and the Ugly,*" will shed light on the impacts and potential risks of AI-based approaches in HR tasks.

We extend our congratulations to the authors of the accepted papers and express gratitude to all authors who submitted their work, members of the program committee, mentors and mentees who participated in the mentorship program, and the EACL 2024 workshop chairs.

We would like to give special thanks to Megagon Labs for their support of our workshop.

The First NLP4HR Workshop Program Chairs
https://megagon.ai/nlp4hr-2024/

Program Committee

Program Chairs

Estevam Hruschka, Megagon Labs
Thom Lake, Indeed and University of Texas at Austin
Tom Mitchell, Carnegie Mellon University
Naoki Otani, Megagon Labs

Reviewers

Aisha Aijaz, Indraprastha Institute of Information Technology, Delhi
Benjamin Clavié, Bright Network
Yoshinari Fujinuma, AWS AI Labs
Nidhi Goyal, Indraprastha Institute of Information Technology, Delhi
Prakhar Gupta, Google
Sairam Gurajada, Megagon Labs
Bo Kang, Ghent University
Mesut Kaya, Aalborg University Copenhagen
Takashi Kodama, Kyoto University
Kaixin Ma, Tencent AI Lab
Seiji Maekawa, Megagon Labs
Takuya Makino, Megagon Labs
Lorenzo Malandri, University of Milan - Bicocca
Hiroshi Matsuda, Megagon Labs
Sajjadur Rahman, Megagon Labs
Weijie Xu, Amazon
Michiharu Yamashita, Pennsylvania State University
Mike Zhang, IT University of Copenhagen

Mentorship Program - Mentors

Nikita Bhutani, Megagon Labs
Lorenzo Malandri, University of Milan - Bicocca
Pouya Pezeshkpour, Megagon Labs
Rob van der Goot, IT University of Copenhagen

Invited Talk: 1

David Graus
Randstad, University of Amsterdam

March 22nd, 2024 – Time: **08:40 - 09:30 CET** – Room: **Gardjola 3 (Corinthia)**

Bio: David Graus is lead data scientist at Randstad, the global leader in the HR services industry. At Randstad he works with his chapter of data scientists on AI-powered products and services, including algorithmic matching of jobs to job seekers and natural language processing for labor market analysis. Prior to his role at Randstad he worked on news personalization for Het Financieele Dagblad, and the award-winning SMART Radio for BNR Nieuwsradio. David obtained his PhD in Information Retrieval in 2017 at the University of Amsterdam under supervision of prof. dr. Maarten de Rijke, where he worked on semantic search and computational methods for automated understanding of large-scale textual digital traces.

Invited Talk: 2

Marko Grobelnik
Jozef Stefan Institute, OECD, European Union Commission
March 22nd, 2024 – Time: **11:00 - 11:50 CET** – Room: **Gardjola 3 (Corinthia)**

Bio: Marko Grobelnik is an expert researcher in the field of Artificial Intelligence (AI). Focused areas of expertise are Machine Learning, Data/Text/Web Mining, Network Analysis, Semantic Technologies, Deep Text Understanding, and Data Visualization. Marko co-leads the Department for Artificial Intelligence at Jozef Stefan Institute, co-founded UNESCO International Research Center on AI (IRCAI), and is the CEO of Quintelligence.com specialized in solving complex AI tasks for the commercial world. He collaborates with major European academic institutions and major industries such as Bloomberg, British Telecom, European Commission, Microsoft Research, New York Times. Marko is co-author of several books, co-founder of several start-ups and is/was involved into over 50 EU funded research projects in various fields of Artificial Intelligence. Marko represents Slovenia in the OECD AI Committee (AIONE) and in the Council of Europe Committee on AI (CAHAI). In 2016 Marko became Digital Champion of Slovenia at the European Commission.

Invited Talk: 3

Barbara Plank
Ludwig-Maximilians-Universität München, IT University of Copenhagen
March 22nd, 2024 – Time: **13:00 - 13:50 CET** – Room: **Gardjola 3 (Corinthia)**

Bio: Barbara Plank is Full Professor and Chair for AI and Computational Linguistics at Ludwig-Maximilians-Universität München (LMU Munich) and Full professor at the IT University of Copenhagen. Her research focuses on NLP and includes learning under sample selection bias (domain adaptation, transfer learning), annotation bias (human disagreements and human uncertainty), learning from beyond the text, and in general learning under limited supervision. Barbara is the recipient of an ERC Consolidator grant, a Sapere Aude Research Leader grant and an Amazon Research Award. Barbara regularly serves in *ACL committees and is currently president of the Northern European Association for Language Technology.

Invited Talk: 4

Trey Causey
Indeed

March 22nd, 2024 – Time: **16:00 - 16:50 CET** – Room: **Gardjola 3 (Corinthia)**

Bio: Trey Causey is Head of Responsible AI and Senior Director of Data Science at Indeed, where he and his team work to ensure Indeed's use of AI is beneficial to job seekers, employers, and society. As the author of Indeed's responsible AI strategy, he leads an interdisciplinary group of data scientists, engineers, and researchers in tackling the sociotechnical issues of algorithmic, human, and systemic bias. He also is a member of Indeed's Environmental, Social, and Governance leadership team, where he and his colleagues are changing the way the world hires, for good. Prior to Indeed, Trey has led data science teams, machine learning engineering teams, and product teams across the technology industry. Trained as a sociologist at the University of Washington, he confronts challenges in Responsible AI with both a sociological and a technological approach.

Table of Contents

Program

Friday, March 22, 2024

08:30 - 08:40	*Opening Remarks*
08:40 - 09:30	*Invited Talk 1*
09:30 - 10:30	*Oral Presentation Session 1*
10:30 - 11:00	*Break*
11:00 - 11:50	*Invited Talk 2*
11:50 - 12:20	*Oral Presentation Session 2*
12:20 - 13:00	*Lunch*
13:00 - 13:50	*Invited Talk 3*
13:50 - 14:40	*Panel*
14:40 - 15:30	*Poster Session*
15:30 - 16:00	*Break*
16:00 - 16:50	*Invited Talk 4*
16:50 - 17:00	*Closing Remarks*

Deep Learning-based Computational Job Market Analysis: A Survey on Skill Extraction and Classification from Job Postings

Elena Senger[1,3], **Mike Zhang**[2], **Rob van der Goot**[2], **Barbara Plank**[1,2]
[1]MaiNLP, Center for Information and Language Processing, LMU Munich, Germany
[2]Department of Computer Science, IT University of Copenhagen, Denmark
[3]Fraunhofer Center for International Management and Knowledge Economy IMW, Germany
elena.senger@cis.lmu.de, {mikz, robv}@itu.dk, b.plank@lmu.de

Abstract

Recent years have brought significant advances to Natural Language Processing (NLP), which enabled fast progress in the field of *computational job market analysis*. Core tasks in this application domain are *skill extraction and classification* from job postings. Because of its quick growth and its interdisciplinary nature, there is no exhaustive assessment of this emerging field. This survey aims to fill this gap by providing a comprehensive overview of deep learning methodologies, datasets, and terminologies specific to NLP-driven skill extraction and classification. Our comprehensive cataloging of publicly available datasets addresses the lack of consolidated information on dataset creation and characteristics. Finally, the focus on terminology addresses the current lack of consistent definitions for important concepts, such as hard and soft skills, and terms relating to skill extraction and classification.

1 Introduction

Skill extraction and classification has recently been the subject of an increased amount of interest (Zhang et al., 2023; Clavié and Soulié, 2023), which shows in a high number of publications, driven by the advances in natural language processing (NLP) technology. For instance, through large language models (LLMs) the low resource tasks of skill extraction can be approached by using synthetic training data (Clavié and Soulié, 2023; Decorte et al., 2023). Surveys regarding skill extraction are emerging (Khaouja et al., 2021a; Papoutsoglou et al., 2019), nevertheless, a comprehensive overview from an NLP perspective is still lacking—a gap we aim to fill in this survey. Our contributions are:

- Firstly, we aim to address the lack of standardized terminology in the field, bringing clarity to terms like hard and soft skills, as well as phrases related to skill extraction and classification.
- Additionally, this survey is the first to examine various publicly accessible datasets and sheds light on their creation methodologies.
- In contrast to prior surveys, we adopt an NLP-centric focus, with a deep dive into the latest advancements of neural methods for skill extraction and classification.

While prior surveys exists, they focus typically on *Skill count* and *Topic modeling* methods for extracting skills. Skill count is performed manually or by matching n-grams with a skill base. Topic modeling is an unsupervised method utilizing word distributions to identify underlying topics in documents. Due to primary statistical basis and lack of defined skill spans or labels, topic modeling, as well as skill count, methods are not covered in this survey. For further details on skill count, see Khaouja et al. (2021a) and Ternikov (2022), and for topic modeling, please refer to Khaouja et al. (2021a), Ternikov (2022) and Ao et al. (2023).

Research Methodology For our search strategy we used several academic databases including the ACL Anthology, Google Scholar, arXiv, IEEE, ACM, Science Direct, and Springer Link. The primary search terms were "skill extraction" and "job". To refine the search, we added terms like "deep learning", "machine learning", or "natural language processing" to our query for Google Scholar and Science Direct databases. This yielded the inclusion of 26 publications on neural skill extraction from job postings (JPs) that were published before November 2023.

2 Other Surveys

Previous surveys provide a foundation for our survey. Notable contributions include works from the social sciences, in particular, by Napierala and

Proceedings of the First Workshop on Natural Language Processing for Human Resources (NLP4HR 2024), pages 1–15
March 22, 2024

Kvetan (2023) in the "Handbook of Computational Social Science for Policy" (Chapter 13). It focuses on changing skills in a dynamic world from a social science perspective. Moreover, Papoutsoglou et al. (2019) focus on studies regarding the software engineering labor market. Besides JPs, they research other sources like social networks or Q&A sites. Lastly, the survey by Khaouja et al. (2021a) on skill identification from JPs is the closest to this survey. It overviews papers using methodologies such as skill counts, topic modeling, skill embeddings, and other machine learning-based methods. With this survey, we steer away from manual and topic modeling approaches to delve deeply into recent extraction methodologies and deep learning-based innovations.

3 Skill-related Terminology

The terms *skill extraction*, *identification* (Li et al., 2023), *detection* (Beauchemin et al., 2022), *standardization* (Li et al., 2023) and *classification* are used differently, sometimes interchangeably, and describe the same or different tasks. We provide the following definition (See an example in Table 3 in the Appendix):

- **Skill Extraction** (E): as a generic (parent) category for retrieving skill-related information. Skill extraction E : JP $\rightarrow (S)$, where E maps a job posting (JP) to a set of skills S.
- **Skill Identification/Detection** (I): as the process of extracting skills without any predefined labels. It can be represented as I : JP $\rightarrow S$, where skills, especially skill spans, are extracted from JPs. It can also be formalized as a classification problem, I : Span $\rightarrow \{0, 1\}$, to determine whether a given span in a JP represents a skill (1) or not (0).
- **Skill Extraction with Coarse Labels** (E_C): as identifying broader categories of skill spans. It is formalized as E_C : JP $\rightarrow \{SC_1, SC_2, \ldots, SC_n\}$, where each SC_i represents a skill span with a coarse label.
- **Skill Standardization** (Std): as the normalization process of skill terms, formalized as $Std : S \rightarrow S'$, mapping an initial set of skills S to a standardized set S'.
- **Direct Skill Classification** (C_D): as mapping skills to a predefined skill base for assigning fine-grained labels. This process can be formalized as $C_D : S \rightarrow L$, where C_D maps a set of already extracted skills S to a set of fine-grained labels L.
- **Skill Classification with Extraction** (C_E): as mapping JPs to a predefined skill base for assigning fine-grained labels. This process can be formalized as $C_E : JP \rightarrow L$, where C_E maps a set of already extracted skills S entire JP or raw JP snippets to a set of fine-grained labels L.

Given these definitions, the skill extraction step can happen at different levels of **granularity** (of the input). Some works extract skills per JP (E_{JP}, the overall document), per sentence ($E_{sentence}$) or per n-gram (E_{n-gram}). A skill span (E_{span})is a continuous n-gram sequence that capture a skill.

A **skill base** (B) is a knowledge base containing skill entities and terminology. A taxonomy is a hierarchically structured skill base, while ontologies provide a structure via relationships between concepts (Khaouja et al., 2021a). Several works use the term "skill dictionary" for a skill base, most often referring to an unstructured skill base or a list of skills (Gugnani and Misra, 2020; Yao et al., 2022). Two popular publicly-available skill bases, created by domain experts, and are frequently used and maintained are the European Skills, Competences, Qualifications and Occupations (ESCO; le Vrang et al., 2014) taxonomy and the US Occupational Information Network (O*NET; Council et al., 2010). We refer to Khaouja et al. (2021a) for more examples of skill bases.

4 What are Skills? On Skill Definitions

Understanding the concept of a *skill* is pivotal in the field of skill extraction. In this section, we investigate several definitions of skills by various publications and institutions, aiming to identify commonalities and distinctions across different sources, which is crucial for establishing a common ground in this emerging field.

The concept of *skill* can be seen as one broad concept (Green et al., 2022; Wild et al., 2021; Fang et al., 2023) or split into subclasses, with multiple possibilities for the split. In the latest version of the ESCO taxonomy the "skill pillar" is divided into four categories: "Transversal skills", "Skills"," Knowledge" and "Language skills and knowledge".[1] O*NET is structured in six domains

[1] https://esco.ec.europa.eu/en/classification/skill_main

(Council et al., 2010), the domain most fitting for skill extraction from JP is "Worker Requirements". This domain entails four subcategories: basic skills, cross-functional skills, knowledge, and education.[2] But publications considered in this survey that define skills, mainly distinguish between hard and soft skills (Tamburri et al., 2020; Beauchemin et al., 2022; Sayfullina et al., 2018), which is therefore also the separation used in this survey.

Hard Skills Tamburri et al. (2020) delineate hard skills as professional competencies, activities, or knowledge pertinent to organizational functions, processes, and roles, essential for the successful completion of specific tasks. This definition emphasizes the practicality and functionality of hard skills within a professional setting. Aligning with this, the study by Beauchemin et al. (2022) views hard skills as task-oriented technical competencies, drawing upon Lyu and Liu (2021) to define them as formal technical abilities for performing certain tasks. Furthermore, Gugnani and Misra (2020) expand on this perspective by incorporating technological terminologies for skill identification and therefore integrating knowledge as a fundamental component of hard skills.

By incorporating knowledge as a component of hard skills, the definitions of hard skills and knowledge categories of O*NET and ESCO can be combined. O*NET's definition of hard skills states that they are developed abilities that enable learning or knowledge acquisition, coupled with their definition of knowledge as "Organized sets of principles and facts applying in general domains".[3] This comprehensive definition underscores not only technical proficiency but also the ability to adapt and apply knowledge. Similarly, ESCO, referencing the European Qualifications Framework, defines skills as "the ability to apply knowledge and use know-how to complete tasks and solve problems", while defining knowledge as "the outcome of the assimilation of information through learning".[4]

In conclusion, we define hard skills as a wide variety of professional abilities, ranging from measurable technical skills to the more general capacity for learning and effectively applying knowledge. They are quantifiable and teachable competencies, predominantly technical, yet intrinsically linked to the ability to adapt and apply them in diverse professional scenarios.

Soft Skills Sayfullina et al. (2018), referencing the Collins dictionary (HarperCollins Publishers, 2023), views soft skills as innate, non-technical qualities highly sought after in employment, diverging from reliance on acquired knowledge. In a more social context, Tamburri et al. (2020) characterizes soft skills as encompassing personal, emotional, social, or intellectual aspects, further known as behavioral skills or competencies. Echoing this sentiment, Beauchemin et al. (2022), drawing from Lyu and Liu (2021), identifies soft skills as a variety of personal attributes and behaviors crucial for effective workplace interaction, collaboration, and adaptability.

Adding to these perspectives, ESCO characterizes soft skills as *transversal skills*, highlighting their wide applicability across various occupations and sectors and their fundamental role in individual growth.[5] Similarly, O*NET classifies these skills under Cross-Functional Skills, defining them as developed capacities that enhance the performance of activities common across different jobs, encompassing areas like Social Skills and Complex Problem Solving Skills.[6] Both sources underscore the universal relevance of soft skills.

These previous definitions lead to our converged definition that soft skills cover a vast array of personal, social, and intellectual competencies, all of which are indispensable for successful interpersonal engagement and personal development in professional settings.

5 Operationalization of Skill Definitions

In this section, we explore various methodologies for operationalizing skill definitions in skill extraction and classification research.

Using a Skill Base By using a given skill base, a pre-defined definition of the concept of skills is provided by the authors of the skill base. Numerous studies employ established skill bases such as the ESCO taxonomy (Zhang et al., 2023, 2022b; Clavié and Soulié, 2023; Decorte et al., 2023, 2022) or O*NET (Gugnani and Misra, 2020). However, it is often ambiguous whether these studies use

[2] https://www.onetcenter.org/content.html

[3] See footnote 2.

[4] https://esco.ec.europa.eu/en/about-esco/escopedia/escopedia/knowledge and https://esco.ec.europa.eu/en/about-esco/escopedia/escopedia/skill

[5] https://esco.ec.europa.eu/en/about-esco/escopedia/escopedia/transversal-knowledge-skills-and-competences

[6] See footnote 2.

all or only specific subcategories (Li et al., 2023; Decorte et al., 2022; Gugnani and Misra, 2020). Some papers mention explicitly the use of all subclasses (Zhang et al., 2022b,a; Gnehm et al., 2022a) other times it can be inferred from the number of skill spans used (Clavié and Soulié, 2023; Decorte et al., 2023). However, one should note that the interpretations of ESCO definitions differ based on the ESCO version and authors' perspective. Zhang et al. (2022a,b) used ESCO version 1.0 with a different soft skill category than discussed in Section 4 and implemented two labels: "knowledge" aligns with ESCO's "Knowledge" category, and "Skills" as a fusion of the hard and soft skills. In contrast, Colombo et al. (2019) using the same ESCO version, but treat soft skills separate from hard skills. Most of the publications used all subcategories as skills without differentiating (Clavié and Soulié, 2023; Gnehm et al., 2022a; Decorte et al., 2023).

Beyond these, there are other skill bases, such as the Russian professional standard in Botov et al. (2019) or the Chinese Occupation Classification Grand Dictionary used in Cao and Zhang (2021); Cao et al. (2021). Additionally, non-official skill bases exist, like the list of 1K soft skills in (Sayfullina et al., 2018) or LinkedIn's in-house taxonomy for skill extraction (Shi et al., 2020). In general, for transparency and reproducibility, it is helpful to state which subset of fine-grained labels L of the skill base (B) and which skill base version is used.

Leveraging Automated Tools Some studies leverage automated tools like AutoPhrase (Shang et al., 2018) or Microsoft Azure Analytics Service for NER for initial skill term detection, followed by manual verification and refinement (Yao et al., 2022; Kortum et al., 2022). Also Vermeer et al. (2022) extract parts of their training data using an automated tool, while others are taken from a skill base.[7] Lastly, Gugnani and Misra (2020) employ an IBM tool for skill identification, which forms a part of a larger skill identification framework.[8] While some previous work did not apply manual verification (Gugnani and Misra, 2020; Vermeer et al., 2022), we recommend it to reduce automation bias from the tool impacting the data.

Definition through Labeling Domain experts play a crucial role for labeling data and therefore impact how the definition of skills is put into work (Shi et al., 2020; Tamburri et al., 2020; Beauchemin et al., 2022). Tamburri et al. (2020) additionally provide a codebook with skill definitions to address ambiguities. Shi et al. (2020) used next skills identified by hiring experts and skills common among successful applicants as training data. The study by Bhola et al. (2020) treat the companies filing the JPs as domain experts by using their labels (see also Section 6). Besides domain experts, crowd workers and the people writing the guidelines for the workers oftentimes determine which terms are skills. Some studies do not mention who labels the data (Wild et al., 2021; Cao and Zhang, 2021; Botov et al., 2019). We suggest being clear about the labeling process and guidelines, making them public for transparency and re-use/standardization, and using domain experts if possible for accurate labeling.

6 Data

In this section, we provide a comprehensive description of publicly available datasets, with an overview in Table 1.

SAYFULLINA by Sayfullina et al. (2018) is a dataset derived from a publicly available Kaggle dataset, containing JPs from within the UK and representing a variety of sectors.[9] The authors retrieved soft skill spans by exact matching with a list of 1,072 soft skills. Each identified span is accompanied by up to 10 surrounding words. Crowdsourcing was used to determine whether the highlighted skill belongs to a job applicant. To ensure reliability, the workers were tested on a small set of JPs and each snippet was evaluated by at least three workers. This process led to a dataset with high class imbalance due to more positive examples. To counter this, additional skill spans were added, including those usually not describing candidates (marked as negative) and those consistently labeled positive.

GREEN by Green et al. (2022) uses the same Kaggle dataset as SAYFULLINA. The labeling was done via crowdsourcing, they did not use experts but only workers who passed a test were included, and encouraged to follow the guidelines. Apart from the "Skill" label capturing hard and soft skills, the labels "Occupation", "Domain", "Experience", "Qualification", and "None" are used in a

[7] https://www.textkernel.com/de/

[8] https://www.ibm.com/products/natural-language-understanding

[9] https://www.kaggle.com/datasets/airiddha/trainrev1/?select=Train_rev1.csv

Publication	Approach	Granularity	Skill type	Use case	Size	📘
(Sayfullina et al., 2018)	Crowdsourced	span-level	soft	I	7411 spans	✖
(Green et al., 2022)	Crowdsourced	span-level	hard + soft	E_C	10,606 spans	✔
(Beauchemin et al., 2022)	Expert	span-level	soft	E_C	47 JPs - 932 spans	✖
(Zhang et al., 2022a)	Expert	span-level	hard + soft	E_C	265 JP - 9,633 spans	✔
(Zhang et al., 2022b)	Expert	span-level	hard + soft	E_C+C_D	60 JP - 920 spans	✔
(Decorte et al., 2022)	Manual	span-level	hard + soft	I+C_D	1,618 spans	✔
(Gnehm et al., 2022b)	Expert	span-level	hard + soft	E_C+C_D	10,995 spans	✖
(Bhola et al., 2020)	Skill Inventory	document-level	unknown	C_E	20,298 JP	✖

Table 1: Overview of publicly-available labeled datasets. 📘 indicates if the authors used guidelines (not necessarily publicly available).

BIO scheme. The authors reduced errors by label aggregation with a preference towards labels from higher-performing workers. Additionally, they reclassified specific "Experience" spans, as "Skill" spans, and manually split multi-term spans into separate spans.

FIJO by Beauchemin et al. (2022) was created in partnership with Canadian insurance companies, and consists of cleaned and de-identified French JPs published between 2009 and 2020. The dataset focus on soft skills and includes 867 JPs with 47 annotated JPs, selected and annotated by a domain expert. The annotated spans are unevenly distributed across four classes: "Thoughts", "Results", "Relational", and "Personal".

SKILLSPAN by Zhang et al. (2022a) consists of the anonymized raw data and annotations of skill and knowledge spans from three JP datasets, one of which cannot be made publicly available due to its license. The available datasets are:

- **HOUSE**: A static in-house dataset with different types of JPs from 2012-2020 and
- **TECH**: The StackOverflow JP platform, consisting mostly of technical jobs collected between June 2020 and September 2021.

The development of the publicly available annotation guidelines involved an iterative process, starting with a few JPs and progressing through several rounds of annotation and refinement by three domain experts.

KOMPETENCER by Zhang et al. (2022b) consists of Danish JPs with annotated skill and knowledge spans, see Table 4 in the Appendix. The same skill definitions, guidelines, and metrics as in SKILLSPAN are used for annotation. This dataset can be used for skill extraction with coarse labels, but the authors have also added fine-grained annotations to evaluate a classification with the ESCO taxonomy. For fine-grained annotations, they query the ESCO API with the annotated spans and use Levenshtein distance to determine the relevance of each obtained label. Then, the quality of these distantly supervised labels is assessed through human evaluation. They also repeated this process for the English SKILLSPAN dataset but only manually checked a sample for calculating statistics.

DECORTE by Decorte et al. (2022) is a variant of the SKILLSPAN dataset with annotated ESCO labels. They used the identified skill without the skill and knowledge labels, but they can be recreated by matching the dataset with SKILLSPAN, see Table 4 in the Appendix. Unlike in KOMPETENCER they manually matched the skills with fitting ESCO labels (if they exist) to create a gold standard.

GNEHM-ICT by Gnehm et al. (2022b) is a Swiss-German dataset where they annotated for Information and Communications Technology (ICT)-related entity recognition. These could be ICT tasks, technology stack, responsibilities, and so forth. The used dataset is a combination of two other Swiss datasets namely the Swiss Job Market Monitor and an online job ad dataset (Gnehm and Clematide, 2020; Buchmann et al., 2022). There are around 25,000 sentences in the dataset.

BHOLA by Bhola et al. (2020) was obtained from a government website[10] in Singapore. The preprocessing steps for this English language dataset include converting text to lowercase and removing stop words and rarely used words. The companies filing the JPs added skill labels, which are mapped to the whole JP document. This makes the dataset suitable for performing multi-label classification by predicting a set of required skills for a given JP.

[10] https://www.mycareersfuture.gov.sg/.

7 Methods

In this section, we survey methods for skill extraction and classification. As in Section 3 the goal of the extraction is to identify skill spans with (E_C) or without coarse labels (I). The classification section covers direct classification methods (C_D) and classification methods with extraction (C_E), both aim to retrieve fine-grained skill labels.

7.1 Skill Extraction

This chapter delineates the evolution of skill extraction methodologies, grouped into three categories: skill identification as span labeling, skill identification through binary classification, and skill extraction with coarse span labels. Starting with LSTM neural networks in 2018 the methods in all three sub-chapters used after the introduction of BERT (Devlin et al., 2019) in 2019 heavily BERT and BERT-based models. Recent advancements continue to diversify the landscape, integrating a broader array of language models (LMs).

7.1.1 Skill Identification as Span Labeling

In this category approach skill identification as a span labeling task. The primary objective is to accurately identify skill spans, encompassing both the identification of the relevant skill phrases and their precise boundaries. Jia et al. (2018) are the first to use sequence tagging for identifying skills from JPs in 2018. The authors use a pre-trained LSTM neural network (Lample et al., 2016) for identifying skill terms on the word-level. Tamburri et al. (2020) also employed binary classification, but at the sentence-level, using a Dutch JP dataset. Their best-performing model, BERT Multilingual Cased, was fine-tuned on expert-annotated JP sentences, suggesting potential improvement with more data and optimization. Further publications retrieve embeddings using a pre-trained BERT model (Wild et al., 2021; Cao and Zhang, 2021; Cao et al., 2021). Notably, Cao et al. (2021) and Cao and Zhang (2021) combine BERT's pre-trained vectors with a Bi-LSTM and a CRF layer for finer entity classification. This approach aligns with previous research demonstrating the efficacy of a CRF layer in NER tasks (Souza et al., 2020). In Zhang et al. (2023), they further built upon the domain-adaptive pre-training paradigm (Gururangan et al., 2020). They make use of the ESCO taxonomy (le Vrang et al., 2014) and integrate this in a multilingual XLM-R model (Conneau et al., 2020), using this taxonomy-driven pre-training method, they introduce a new state-of-the-art for all skill identification benchmarks. For analysis, they show that performance increases especially for skills that are shorter in length, due to ESCO skills also being shorter.

In contrast to these single-model approaches, Gugnani and Misra (2020) adopted a multi-faceted methodology to predict the relevance of identified skill spans. Their methodology encompassed four modules: using part-of-speech (PoS) tagging, parsing sentences with skill bases (O*NET, Hope, and Wikipedia), leveraging a ready-made sequence tagging solution, and employing a pre-trained word2vec model for final score determination through cosine similarity.[11]

7.1.2 Skill Identification as binary Classification Task

In this category, skill identification is framed as a binary classification task. The focus is on determining whether a given sequence either constitutes or contains a (specific) skill. The task in Sayfullina et al. (2018) differs from the other publications. They extract skill spans by exact match and aim to decide whether skill spans refer to a candidate or something else, like a company. They experiment with various classifiers and input representations, such as Soft Skill Masking, Embedding, and Tagging, finding the LSTM classifier with skill tagging most effective on their dataset. Tamburri et al. (2020) employed binary classification at the sentence-level to determine if it contains a skill. Their best-performing model, BERT Multilingual Cased, was fine-tuned on expert-annotated JP sentences using a Dutch JP dataset. Yao et al. (2022) classify individual words as skill-related or not. They split JPs into individual words, analyzing each through character-level and word-level encoders, integrating linguistic features like POS tags and capitalization. Their initial training employs AutoPhrase (Shang et al., 2018) for automatic skill term identification, followed by manual verification and expert-labeled samples. The model is further refined using Positive-Unlabeled learning, where the classifier's predictions on unlabeled data help expand the skill base for continuous adaptation.

[11] https://www.ibm.com/products/natural-language-understanding.

Paper	Model	Skill Type	Granularity	Use Case
(Fang et al., 2023)	Custom pre-trained LM	soft + hard	word-level	E_C
(Goyal et al., 2023)	FastText skip-gram, GNN	unknown	word-level	C_E
(Clavié and Soulié, 2023)	GPT-4	soft + hard	span-level	C_E
(Li et al., 2023)	XMLC - LLM	soft + hard	document-level	C_E
(Decorte et al., 2023)	GPT-3.5	soft + hard	sentence-level	C_E
(Zhang et al., 2023)	Multilingual XLM-R	soft + hard	span-level	E_C
(Decorte et al., 2022)	RoBERTa	soft + hard	sentence-level	C_E
(Zhang et al., 2022c)	RoBERTa, JobBERT	soft + hard	span-level	C_D
(Gnehm et al., 2022a)	JobBERT-de, SBERT	soft + hard	span-level	$E_C + C_D$
(Zhang et al., 2022b)	BERTbase , DaBERT	soft + hard	span-level	C_E
(Beauchemin et al., 2022)	Bi-LSTM, CamemBERT	soft	span-level	E_C
(Yao et al., 2022)	BERT, word2vec	unknown	word-level	I
(Anand et al., 2022)	LaBSE model	soft + hard	title	C_E
(Vermeer et al., 2022)	RobBERT	soft + hard	document-level	C_E
(Wild et al., 2021)	BERT, spaCy	soft + hard	span-level	I
(Khaouja et al., 2021b)	Sent2vec, SBERT	soft + hard	sentence-level	C_E
(Cao et al., 2021)	BERT-BiLSTM-CRF	soft + hard	span-level	I
(Cao and Zhang, 2021)	BERT-BiLSTM-CRF	soft + hard	span-level	I
(Li et al., 2020)	Deep Averaging Network, FastText	unknown	span-level	C_E
(Tamburri et al., 2020)	BERT Multilingual Cased	soft + hard	sentence-level	I
(Bhola et al., 2020)	BERTbase	unknown	document-level	C_E
(Gugnani and Misra, 2020)	Word2vec	soft + hard	span-level	I
(Botov et al., 2019)	Word2vec	unknown	span-level	C_E
(Jia et al., 2018)	LSTM	unknown	word-level	I
(Sayfullina et al., 2018)	CNN, LSTM, HAN	soft	span-level	I
(Javed et al., 2017)	Word2vec	soft + hard	span-level	C_E

Table 2: Publications regarding neural skill extraction and classification. The skill type was not always explicitly mentioned in some cases it's derived from examples given in the paper.

7.1.3 Skill Extraction with Coarse Labels

This section explores advancements in skill extraction with coarse labels, where each publication extract spans from two to four different categories. The studies of Gnehm et al. (2022a) and Zhang et al. (2022a) both utilize sequence tagging-based models. Gnehm et al. (2022a) focusing on iterative training and annotation with jobBERT-de, a German LM tailored for JPs. Zhang et al. (2022a) compare BERT-based (Devlin et al., 2019) and SpanBERT-based (Joshi et al., 2020) models, highlighting the importance of domain adaptation. On the other hand, Beauchemin et al. (2022) and Fang et al. (2023) delve into the intricacies of training and optimizing LMs for skill extraction. Beauchemin et al. (2022) examine the sensitivity of Bi-LSTM and CamemBERT (Martin et al., 2020) models to training data volume, with CamemBERT unfrozen yielding the highest mean token-wise accuracy. Fang et al. (2023) introduce RecruitPro, a specialized model for skill extraction from recruitment texts, employing innovative techniques for dealing with data noise and label imbalances. Collectively, these papers emphasize the need for tailored approaches and continuous innovation in model development.

7.2 Skill Classification

While skill standardization can be achieved through classification, other methods such as clustering (Bernabé-Moreno et al., 2019; Lukauskas et al., 2023), matching n-grams based on string similarity (Boselli et al., 2018), or identifying semantically similar skills (Bernabé-Moreno et al., 2019; Colombo et al., 2019; Grüger and Schneider, 2019) also lead to standardized skill spans. These methods simplify the variety and quantity of skill spans without assigning standardized labels. Transitioning from these methods, we now focus on skill classification, a crucial step for assigning standardized labels to effectively organize and understand skills. Most publications skip a traditional extraction and match the JPs directly to the skill base (C_E), which can be seen as skill extraction against a skill base. Exceptions are Gnehm et al. (2022a), which perform extraction of skill spans with coarse labels before the fine-grained classification step, and Zhang et al. (2022b) who rely on prior work for extraction and focus solely on the matching of skill spans to ESCO (C_D). We divide the publications by methodology into those that match based on semantic similarity and those using extreme multi-label classification to solve the matching task.

7.2.1 Similarity-based Approaches

The publications with similarity-based approaches split the JPs into sentences or n-grams before matching them. All of the following publications use skill embedding methods, which can be seen as an advancement of the skill count methods (Section 1). The advances in text embeddings over time are reflected in the scope of the approaches. While Javed et al. (2017) and Botov et al. (2019) improve the matching using word2vec embeddings(Mikolov et al., 2013), later Li et al. (2020) use FastText (Bojanowski et al., 2017) leveraging sub-word information to handle out-of-vocabulary words and capture more detailed semantic and syntactic information. Khaouja et al. (2021b) compare using sent2vec trained on Wikipedia sentences, and SBERT (Reimers and Gurevych, 2019) trained on millions of paraphrase sentences for embeddings. Moreover, Zhang et al. (2022c) uses LMs like RoBERTa and JobBERT to match n-grams from JP sentences with the ESCO taxonomy. They also experiment with context and frequency-aware embeddings. Gnehm et al. (2022a) performed direct skill extraction using context-aware embeddings and the SBERT model similar to Zhang et al. (2022c), additionally they contextualize skill areas within spans and ontology terms using their hierarchical structure. The study explores techniques to enhance BERT model similarity, including in-domain pretraining, transformer-based sequential denoising auto-encoder (TSDAE; Wang et al., 2021) for domain-specific terminology, and Siamese BERT Networks for training sentence embeddings (Reimers and Gurevych, 2019). They further leverage MNR loss in Siamese networks (Henderson et al., 2017), using ontology data to create positive text pairings for better label matching. SkillGPT (Li et al., 2023) is the first tool to use an LLM for the matching task, they convert ESCO entries into structured documents, which are vectorized by the LM. Then, they summarize the input text, and use an embedding of the summary to retrieve the closest ESCO entries.

7.2.2 Extreme Multi-label Classification Approaches

Bhola et al. (2020) were the first to formulate skill extraction against a skill base as an extreme multi-label classification (XMLC). They classify multiple skill labels per document using the labels of the BHOLA dataset (around 2500 labels) as a skill base. Their BERT–XMLC framework, involves a Text Encoder that uses the pre-trained BERTbase model to convert JP texts into dense vector representations, a Bottleneck Layer that reduces overfitting by compressing these representations (Liu et al., 2017) and subsequently a fully connected layer for multi-label classification of the skills. Enhancements include focusing on semantic skill label representation and skill co-occurrence, using bootstrapping to augment training data, and improve skill correlation capture. Their model outperformed XMLC baselines. Vermeer et al. (2022) adapted this approach for using RobBERT and additional linear layers, validating on BHOLA and a non-public Dutch dataset. Similarly, Anand et al. (2022) extended the model to predict skill importance using LaBSE-encoded (Feng et al., 2022) job titles, ranking skills from an in-house database based on a 0-1 scale of importance.

Subsequent publications have concentrated on XMLC for skill extraction and classification using the ESCO taxonomy with around 13000 labels. For a pure skill classification for already identified skill spans Zhang et al. (2022b) use distant supervision by querying the ESCO API for the fine-grained skill labels. For model training, they employ zero-shot cross-lingual transfer learning techniques using various BERT models and fine-tune them on Danish JPs. The effectiveness of the models is tested on an adapted version of SKILLSPAN and KOMPETENCER. The same year Decorte et al. (2022) addressed the XMLC task on the sentence-level, again using distant supervision with the ESCO taxonomy. They enhance binary skill classifier training with three negative sampling strategies, involving siblings in ESCO hierarchy, Levenshtein distance, and cosine similarity of RoBERTa-encoded skill names. Their model employs a frozen pre-trained RoBERTa with mean pooling for sentence representation, followed by separate binary classifiers for each skill, evaluated on DECORTE.

As for the similarity-based approaches, LLMs are prominent in recent XMLC approaches. Unlike Li et al. (2023), Decorte et al. (2023) use the LLM solely during training to reduce latency and enhance reproducibility. They create a synthetic training dataset using the LLM, then optimize a bi-encoder through contrastive training, to effectively represent both skill names and corresponding sentences in close proximity within the same space. This method outperforms the distance supervision baseline by Decorte et al. (2022) (see Table 5). Similarly, Clavié and Soulié (2023) treat the skill extraction and classification task as individual binary classification problems, using GPT-3.5 like Decorte et al. (2023) but generating more spans per skill for synthetic training. They propose two extraction methods: one using linear classifiers for each skill, employing hard negative sampling (Robinson et al., 2021) for improved skill differentiation, and another based on similarity, utilizing E5-LARGE-V2 embeddings (Wang et al., 2022) for cosine similarity calculations between JP extracts and ESCO labels or synthetic sentences. Potential skills are then reranked using an LLM. In evaluations using the DECORTE dataset, their methods achieved high performance with GPT-4, though results with GPT-3.5 were lower than Decorte et al. (2023), see Table 5 in the Appendix.

Goyal et al. (2023) present JobXMLC, a unique framework for the XMLC task, distinct from the prevailing methods. JobXMLC integrates a job-skill graph to represent job-skill interconnections, utilizes a GNN for multi-hop embeddings from the graph's structure, and incorporates an extreme classification system with skill attention based on skill frequency in the dataset. The framework's effectiveness is validated on the BHOLA and a proprietary StackOverflow dataset, see Table 5 in the Appendix.

8 Conclusions and Future Directions

Recent publications indicate two emerging trends in skill extraction. Firstly, extracting skills against skill bases like ESCO is gaining popularity, facilitating cross-industry and regional comparisons. Secondly, LLMs are increasingly applied in skill extraction and classification, proving particularly advantageous due to the scarcity of training data in this domain.

Future research in skill extraction and classification could focus on emerging skills and the extraction of implicit skills. Methods like those by Javed et al. (2017) and Khaouja et al. (2021b) update skill bases with emerging technologies and frequently used keywords, but evaluating these remains difficult without a standard benchmark. The challenge of extracting implicit skills, not directly stated in job postings, is also gaining attention. Techniques include prompting LLMs to generate training data with implied skills (Clavié and Soulié, 2023) and using complete sentences to encompass both explicit and implicit skills (Decorte et al., 2022, 2023). However, these methods need thorough evaluation, presenting an open field for future exploration.

Limitations

A limitation that should be considered is that only publications in the English language (although data was from multiple languages) were surveyed in this paper. Second, to allow for a deeper focus publications regarding topic modeling were excluded even if they used deep-learning-based methods.

Acknowledgements

We thank the reviewers for their insightful feedback. ES acknowledges financial support with funds provided by the German Federal Ministry for Economic Affairs and Climate Action due to an enactment of the German Bundestag under grant 46SKD127X (GENESIS). MZ is supported by the Independent Research Fund Denmark (DFF) grant 9131-00019B and BP is supported by ERC Consolidator Grant DIALECT 101043235.

References

Sarthak Anand, Jens-Joris Decorte, and Niels Lowie. 2022. Is it required? ranking the skills required for a job-title.

Ziqiao Ao, Gergely Horváth, Chunyuan Sheng, Yifan Song, and Yutong Sun. 2023. Skill requirements in job advertisements: A comparison of skill-categorization methods based on wage regressions. *Information Processing & Management*, 60(2):103185.

David Beauchemin, Julien Laumonier, Yvan Le Ster, and Marouane Yassine. 2022. "fijo": a french insurance soft skill detection dataset.

Juan Bernabé-Moreno, Álvaro Tejeda-Lorente, Julio Herce-Zelaya, Carlos Porcel, and Enrique Herrera-Viedma. 2019. An automatic skills standardization method based on subject expert knowledge extraction and semantic matching. *Procedia Computer Science*, 162:857–864. 7th International Conference on Information Technology and Quantitative Management (ITQM 2019): Information technology and quantitative management based on Artificial Intelligence.

Akshay Bhola, Kishaloy Halder, Animesh Prasad, and Min-Yen Kan. 2020. Retrieving skills from job descriptions: A language model based extreme multi-label classification framework. In *Proceedings of the 28th International Conference on Computational Linguistics*, pages 5832–5842, Barcelona, Spain (Online). International Committee on Computational Linguistics.

Piotr Bojanowski, Edouard Grave, Armand Joulin, and Tomas Mikolov. 2017. Enriching word vectors with subword information. *Transactions of the Association for Computational Linguistics*, 5:135–146.

Roberto Boselli, Mirko Cesarini, Fabio Mercorio, and Mario Mezzanzanica. 2018. Classifying online job advertisements through machine learning. *Future Generation Computer Systems*, 86:319–328.

Dmitriy Botov, Julius Klenin, Andrey Melnikov, Yuri Dmitrin, Ivan Nikolaev, and Mikhail Vinel. 2019. Mining labor market requirements using distributional semantic models and deep learning. In *Business Information Systems - 22nd International Conference, BIS 2019, Seville, Spain, June 26-28, 2019, Proceedings, Part II*, volume 354 of *Lecture Notes in Business Information Processing*, pages 177–190. Springer.

Marlis Buchmann, Helen Buchs, Felix Busch, Simon Clematide, Ann-Sophie Gnehm, and Jan Müller. 2022. Swiss job market monitor: A rich source of demand-side micro data of the labour market. *European Sociological Review*.

Lina Cao and Jian Zhang. 2021. Skill requirements analysis for data analysts based on named entities recognition. In *2021 2nd International Conference on Big Data and Informatization Education (ICBDIE)*, pages 64–68.

Lina Cao, Jian Zhang, Xinquan Ge, and Jindong Chen. 2021. Occupational profiling driven by online job advertisements: Taking the data analysis and processing engineering technicians as an example. *PLoS ONE*, 16.

Benjamin Clavié and Guillaume Soulié. 2023. Large language models as batteries-included zero-shot esco skills matchers.

Emilio Colombo, Fabio Mercorio, and Mario Mezzanzanica. 2019. Ai meets labor market: Exploring the link between automation and skills. *Information Economics and Policy*, 47:27–37. The Economics of Artificial Intelligence and Machine Learning.

Alexis Conneau, Kartikay Khandelwal, Naman Goyal, Vishrav Chaudhary, Guillaume Wenzek, Francisco Guzmán, Edouard Grave, Myle Ott, Luke Zettlemoyer, and Veselin Stoyanov. 2020. Unsupervised cross-lingual representation learning at scale. In *Proceedings of the 58th Annual Meeting of the Association for Computational Linguistics*, pages 8440–8451, Online. Association for Computational Linguistics.

National Research Council, Nancy Thomas Tippins, Margaret L Hilton, et al. 2010. *A database for a changing economy: Review of the Occupational Information Network (O* NET)*. National Academies Press.

Jens-Joris Decorte, Jeroen Van Hautte, Johannes Deleu, Chris Develder, and Thomas Demeester. 2022. Design of negative sampling strategies for distantly supervised skill extraction. In *Proceedings of the 2nd Workshop on Recommender Systems for Human Resources (RecSys-in-HR 2022)*, volume 3218, page 7. CEUR.

Jens-Joris Decorte, Severine Verlinden, Jeroen Van Hautte, Johannes Deleu, Chris Develder, and Thomas Demeester. 2023. Extreme multi-label skill extraction training using large language models.

Jacob Devlin, Ming-Wei Chang, Kenton Lee, and Kristina Toutanova. 2019. BERT: Pre-training of deep bidirectional transformers for language understanding. In *Proceedings of the 2019 Conference of the North American Chapter of the Association for Computational Linguistics: Human Language Technologies, Volume 1 (Long and Short Papers)*, pages 4171–4186, Minneapolis, Minnesota. Association for Computational Linguistics.

Chuyu Fang, Chuan Qin, Qi Zhang, Kaichun Yao, Jingshuai Zhang, Hengshu Zhu, Fuzhen Zhuang, and Hui Xiong. 2023. Recruitpro: A pretrained language model with skill-aware prompt learning for intelligent recruitment. In *Proceedings of the 29th ACM SIGKDD Conference on Knowledge Discovery and Data Mining*, KDD '23, page 3991–4002, New York, NY, USA. Association for Computing Machinery.

Fangxiaoyu Feng, Yinfei Yang, Daniel Cer, Naveen Arivazhagan, and Wei Wang. 2022. Language-agnostic BERT sentence embedding. In *Proceedings of the 60th Annual Meeting of the Association for Computational Linguistics (Volume 1: Long Papers)*, pages 878–891, Dublin, Ireland. Association for Computational Linguistics.

Ann-sophie Gnehm, Eva Bühlmann, Helen Buchs, and Simon Clematide. 2022a. Fine-grained extraction and classification of skill requirements in German-speaking job ads. In *Proceedings of the Fifth Workshop on Natural Language Processing and Computational Social Science (NLP+CSS)*, pages 14–24, Abu Dhabi, UAE. Association for Computational Linguistics.

Ann-Sophie Gnehm, Eva Bühlmann, and Simon Clematide. 2022b. Evaluation of transfer learning and domain adaptation for analyzing German-speaking job advertisements. In *Proceedings of the Thirteenth Language Resources and Evaluation Conference*, pages 3892–3901, Marseille, France. European Language Resources Association.

Ann-Sophie Gnehm and Simon Clematide. 2020. Text zoning and classification for job advertisements in German, French and English. In *Proceedings of the Fourth Workshop on Natural Language Processing and Computational Social Science*, pages 83–93, Online. Association for Computational Linguistics.

Nidhi Goyal, Jushaan Kalra, Charu Sharma, Raghava Mutharaju, Niharika Sachdeva, and Ponnurangam

Kumaraguru. 2023. JobXMLC: EXtreme multi-label classification of job skills with graph neural networks. In *Findings of the Association for Computational Linguistics: EACL 2023*, pages 2181–2191, Dubrovnik, Croatia. Association for Computational Linguistics.

Thomas Green, Diana Maynard, and Chenghua Lin. 2022. Development of a benchmark corpus to support entity recognition in job descriptions. In *Proceedings of the Thirteenth Language Resources and Evaluation Conference*, pages 1201–1208, Marseille, France. European Language Resources Association.

Joscha Grüger and Georg Schneider. 2019. Automated analysis of job requirements for computer scientists in online job advertisements. In *Proceedings of the 15th International Conference on Web Information Systems and Technologies*, WEBIST 2019, page 226–233, Setubal, PRT. SCITEPRESS - Science and Technology Publications, Lda.

Akshay Gugnani and Hemant Misra. 2020. Implicit skills extraction using document embedding and its use in job recommendation. In *The Thirty-Fourth AAAI Conference on Artificial Intelligence, AAAI 2020, The Thirty-Second Innovative Applications of Artificial Intelligence Conference, IAAI 2020, The Tenth AAAI Symposium on Educational Advances in Artificial Intelligence, EAAI 2020, New York, NY, USA, February 7-12, 2020*, pages 13286–13293. AAAI Press.

Suchin Gururangan, Ana Marasović, Swabha Swayamdipta, Kyle Lo, Iz Beltagy, Doug Downey, and Noah A. Smith. 2020. Don't stop pretraining: Adapt language models to domains and tasks. In *Proceedings of the 58th Annual Meeting of the Association for Computational Linguistics*, pages 8342–8360, Online. Association for Computational Linguistics.

HarperCollins Publishers. 2023. Collins COBUILD Advanced Learner's Dictionary: Soft Skills. `https://www.collinsdictionary.com/dictionary/english/soft-skills`.

Matthew Henderson, Rami Al-Rfou, Brian Strope, Yun hsuan Sung, Laszlo Lukacs, Ruiqi Guo, Sanjiv Kumar, Balint Miklos, and Ray Kurzweil. 2017. Efficient natural language response suggestion for smart reply.

Faizan Javed, Phuong Hoang, Thomas Mahoney, and Matt McNair. 2017. Large-scale occupational skills normalization for online recruitment. In *Proceedings of the AAAI Conference on Artificial Intelligence*, volume 31, pages 4627–4634.

Shanshan Jia, Xiaoan Liu, Ping Zhao, Chang Liu, Lianying Sun, and Tao Peng. 2018. Representation of job-skill in artificial intelligence with knowledge graph analysis. In *2018 IEEE symposium on product compliance engineering-asia (ISPCE-CN)*, pages 1–6. IEEE.

Mandar Joshi, Danqi Chen, Yinhan Liu, Daniel S. Weld, Luke Zettlemoyer, and Omer Levy. 2020. SpanBERT: Improving pre-training by representing and predicting spans. *Transactions of the Association for Computational Linguistics*, 8:64–77.

Imane Khaouja, Ismail Kassou, and Mounir Ghogho. 2021a. A survey on skill identification from online job ads. *IEEE Access*, 9:118134–118153.

Imane Khaouja, Ghita Mezzour, and Ismail Kassou. 2021b. Unsupervised skill identification from job ads. In *2021 IEEE 22nd International Conference on Information Reuse and Integration for Data Science (IRI)*, pages 147–151.

Henrik Kortum, Jonas Rebstadt, and Oliver Thomas. 2022. Dissection of AI job advertisements: A text mining-based analysis of employee skills in the disciplines computer vision and natural language processing. In *55th Hawaii International Conference on System Sciences, HICSS 2022, Virtual Event / Maui, Hawaii, USA, January 4-7, 2022*, pages 1–10. ScholarSpace.

Guillaume Lample, Miguel Ballesteros, Sandeep Subramanian, Kazuya Kawakami, and Chris Dyer. 2016. Neural architectures for named entity recognition. In *Proceedings of the 2016 Conference of the North American Chapter of the Association for Computational Linguistics: Human Language Technologies*, pages 260–270, San Diego, California. Association for Computational Linguistics.

Martin le Vrang, Agis Papantoniou, Erika Pauwels, Pieter Fannes, Dominique Vandensteen, and Johan De Smedt. 2014. Esco: Boosting job matching in europe with semantic interoperability. *Computer*, 47(10):57–64.

Nan Li, Bo Kang, and Tijl De Bie. 2023. Skillgpt: a restful api service for skill extraction and standardization using a large language model.

Shan Li, Baoxu Shi, Jaewon Yang, Ji Yan, Shuai Wang, Fei Chen, and Qi He. 2020. Deep job understanding at linkedin. In *Proceedings of the 43rd International ACM SIGIR conference on research and development in Information Retrieval, SIGIR 2020, Virtual Event, China, July 25-30, 2020*, pages 2145–2148. ACM.

Jingzhou Liu, Wei-Cheng Chang, Yuexin Wu, and Yiming Yang. 2017. Deep learning for extreme multi-label text classification. In *Proceedings of the 40th International ACM SIGIR Conference on Research and Development in Information Retrieval, Shinjuku, Tokyo, Japan, August 7-11, 2017*, pages 115–124. ACM.

Mantas Lukauskas, Viktorija Šarkauskaitė, Vaida Pilinkienė, Alina Stundziene, Andrius Grybauskas, and Jurgita Bruneckienė. 2023. Enhancing skills demand understanding through job ad segmentation using nlp and clustering techniques. *Applied Sciences*, 13.

Wenjing Lyu and Jin Liu. 2021. Soft skills, hard skills: What matters most? evidence from job postings. *Applied Energy*, 300:117307.

Louis Martin, Benjamin Muller, Pedro Javier Ortiz Suárez, Yoann Dupont, Laurent Romary, Éric de la Clergerie, Djamé Seddah, and Benoît Sagot. 2020. CamemBERT: a tasty French language model. In *Proceedings of the 58th Annual Meeting of the Association for Computational Linguistics*, pages 7203–7219, Online. Association for Computational Linguistics.

Tomas Mikolov, Kai Chen, Greg Corrado, and Jeffrey Dean. 2013. Efficient estimation of word representations in vector space.

Joanna Napierala and Vladimir Kvetan. 2023. *Changing Job Skills in a Changing World*, pages 243–259. Springer International Publishing, Cham.

Maria Papoutsoglou, Apostolos Ampatzoglou, Nikolaos Mittas, and Lefteris Angelis. 2019. Extracting knowledge from on-line sources for software engineering labor market: A mapping study. *IEEE Access*, 7:157595–157613.

Nils Reimers and Iryna Gurevych. 2019. Sentence-BERT: Sentence embeddings using Siamese BERT-networks. In *Proceedings of the 2019 Conference on Empirical Methods in Natural Language Processing and the 9th International Joint Conference on Natural Language Processing (EMNLP-IJCNLP)*, pages 3982–3992, Hong Kong, China. Association for Computational Linguistics.

Joshua David Robinson, Ching-Yao Chuang, Suvrit Sra, and Stefanie Jegelka. 2021. Contrastive learning with hard negative samples. In *9th International Conference on Learning Representations, ICLR 2021, Virtual Event, Austria, May 3-7, 2021*. OpenReview.net.

Luiza Sayfullina, Eric Malmi, and Juho Kannala. 2018. Learning representations for soft skill matching. In *Analysis of Images, Social Networks and Texts*, pages 141–152, Cham. Springer International Publishing.

Jingbo Shang, Jialu Liu, Meng Jiang, Xiang Ren, Clare R. Voss, and Jiawei Han. 2018. Automated phrase mining from massive text corpora. *IEEE Transactions on Knowledge and Data Engineering*, 30(10):1825–1837.

Baoxu Shi, Jaewon Yang, Feng Guo, and Qi He. 2020. Salience and market-aware skill extraction for job targeting. In *KDD '20: The 26th ACM SIGKDD Conference on Knowledge Discovery and Data Mining, Virtual Event, CA, USA, August 23-27, 2020*, pages 2871–2879. ACM.

Fábio Souza, Rodrigo Nogueira, and Roberto Lotufo. 2020. Portuguese named entity recognition using bert-crf.

Damian A. Tamburri, Willem-Jan Van Den Heuvel, and Martin Garriga. 2020. Dataops for societal intelligence: a data pipeline for labor market skills extraction and matching. In *2020 IEEE 21st International Conference on Information Reuse and Integration for Data Science (IRI)*, pages 391–394.

Andrei Ternikov. 2022. Soft and hard skills identification: insights from it job advertisements in the cis region.

Ninande Vermeer, Vera Provatorova, David Graus, Thilina Rajapakse, and Sepideh Mesbah. 2022. Using robbert and extreme multi-label classification to extract implicit and explicit skills from dutch job descriptions. In *compjobs '22: Computational Jobs Marketplace, Feb 25, 2022*. ACM.

Kexin Wang, Nils Reimers, and Iryna Gurevych. 2021. TSDAE: Using transformer-based sequential denoising auto-encoderfor unsupervised sentence embedding learning. In *Findings of the Association for Computational Linguistics: EMNLP 2021*, pages 671–688, Punta Cana, Dominican Republic. Association for Computational Linguistics.

Liang Wang, Nan Yang, Xiaolong Huang, Binxing Jiao, Linjun Yang, Daxin Jiang, Rangan Majumder, and Furu Wei. 2022. Text embeddings by weakly-supervised contrastive pre-training.

Simon Wild, Soyhan Parlar, Thomas Hanne, and Rolf Dornberger. 2021. Naïve bayes and named entity recognition for requirements mining in job postings. In *2021 3rd International Conference on Natural Language Processing (ICNLP)*, pages 155–161.

Kaichun Yao, Jingshuai Zhang, Chuan Qin, Peng Wang, Hengshu Zhu, and Hui Xiong. 2022. Knowledge enhanced person-job fit for talent recruitment. In *2022 IEEE 38th International Conference on Data Engineering (ICDE)*, pages 3467–3480.

Mike Zhang, Kristian Jensen, Sif Sonniks, and Barbara Plank. 2022a. SkillSpan: Hard and soft skill extraction from English job postings. In *Proceedings of the 2022 Conference of the North American Chapter of the Association for Computational Linguistics: Human Language Technologies*, pages 4962–4984, Seattle, United States. Association for Computational Linguistics.

Mike Zhang, Kristian Nørgaard Jensen, and Barbara Plank. 2022b. Kompetencer: Fine-grained skill classification in Danish job postings via distant supervision and transfer learning. In *Proceedings of the Thirteenth Language Resources and Evaluation Conference*, pages 436–447, Marseille, France. European Language Resources Association.

Mike Zhang, Kristian Nørgaard Jensen, Rob van der Goot, and Barbara Plank. 2022c. Skill extraction from job postings using weak supervision. In *RecSys in HR'22: The 2nd Workshop on Recommender Systems for Human Resources, in conjunction with the 16th ACM Conference on Recommender Systems,*

September 18–23, 2022, Seattle, USA. CEUR Workshop Proceedings.

Mike Zhang, Rob van der Goot, and Barbara Plank. 2023. ESCOXLM-R: Multilingual taxonomy-driven pre-training for the job market domain. In *Proceedings of the 61st Annual Meeting of the Association for Computational Linguistics (Volume 1: Long Papers)*, pages 11871–11890, Toronto, Canada. Association for Computational Linguistics.

A Appendix

A.1 Terminology Example

In Table 3, we present an example sentence for better terminology understanding.

	Familiar	with	building	tests	in	python
I:	O	O	B	I	O	B
E_C:	O	O	B_{skill}	I_{skill}	O	$\text{B}_{knowl.}$
C_D/C_E:	"Python (computer programming)", " plan " "software testing"					

Table 3: An example with annotations for the different tasks described in Section 3. For skill classification (C), we used the ESCO taxonomy in this example, and for skill extraction with coarse labels (E_C) we follow the guidelines of SkillSpan (Zhang et al., 2022a)

A.2 Number of Skill and Knowledge Spans

In Table 4, we show the number of labeled spans for skills and knowledge in the SKILLSPAN (Zhang et al., 2022a), DECORTE (Decorte et al., 2022), and KOMPETENCER (Zhang et al., 2022b) dataset.

A.3 Scores of Selected Models

In Table 5, we display the scores of recent LMM-based approaches on the DECORTE (Decorte et al., 2022) dataset for comparison. Furthermore, we show results of Zhang et al. (2023); Goyal et al. (2023) and (Bhola et al., 2020) on the BHOLA (Bhola et al., 2020) dataset.

Source	# Skill Spans	# Knowledge Spans
SKILLSPAN - HOUSE	2,146	1,418
DECORTE - HOUSE	509*	210*
SKILLSPAN - TECH	2,241	3,828
DECORTE - TECH	419	480*
KOMPETENCER	665	255

Table 4: Number of labeled spans. The star * indicates, that two values found in the Decorte HOUSE test dataset (tagged as knowledge) were actually from the Skillspan TECH dataset; eight values found in the Decorte TECH test dataset (four skill spans, four knowledge spans) were actually from the Skillspan HOUSE dataset.

Model	Source	HOUSE*			TECH*			BHOLA		
		MRR	RP@5	RP@10	MRR	RP@5	RP@10	MRR	R@5	R@10
$Classifier^{neg}$	(Decorte et al., 2022)	0.299	30.82	38.69	0.326	31.71	39.09	N/A	N/A	N/A
$GPTsentences^{aug}$	(Decorte et al., 2023)	0.428	45.74	N/A	0.529	54.62	N/A	N/A	N/A	N/A
$GPT3.5Re-ranking$	(Clavié and Soulié, 2023)	0.427	43.57	51.44	0.488	52.50	59.75	N/A	N/A	N/A
$GPT4Re-ranking$	(Clavié and Soulié, 2023)	0.495	53.34	61.02	0.537	61.50	68.94	N/A	N/A	N/A
$BERT\breve{}XMLC+CAB$	(Bhola et al., 2020)	N/A	N/A	N/A	N/A	N/A	N/A	0.9049	21.67	40.49
$JobXMLC$	(Goyal et al., 2023)	N/A	N/A	N/A	N/A	N/A	N/A	0.90	18.29	32.33
$ESCOXML-R$	(Zhang et al., 2023)	N/A	N/A	N/A	N/A	N/A	N/A	0.907	N/A	N/A

Table 5: Scores of selected models on the benchmarking datasets DECORTE and BHOLA.

Aspect-Based Sentiment Analysis for Open-Ended HR Survey Responses

Lois Rink[*]
Universiteit van Amsterdam
Amsterdam, The Netherlands
Lrink@hotmail.com

Job Meijdam
Randstad Groep Nederland
Diemen, The Netherlands
job.meijdam@randstadgroep.nl

David Graus
Randstad
Diemen, The Netherlands
david.graus@randstad.com

Abstract

Understanding preferences, opinions, and sentiment of the workforce is paramount for effective employee lifecycle management. Open-ended survey responses serve as a valuable source of information. This paper proposes a machine learning approach for aspect-based sentiment analysis (ABSA) of Dutch open-ended responses in employee satisfaction surveys. Our approach aims to overcome the inherent noise and variability in these responses, enabling a comprehensive analysis of sentiments that can support employee lifecycle management. Through response clustering we identify six key aspects (salary, schedule, contact, communication, personal attention, agreements), which we validate by domain experts. We compile a dataset of 1,458 Dutch survey responses, revealing label imbalance in aspects and sentiments. We propose few-shot approaches for ABSA based on Dutch BERT models, and compare them against bag-of-words and zero-shot baselines. Our work significantly contributes to the field of ABSA by demonstrating the first successful application of Dutch pre-trained language models to aspect-based sentiment analysis in the domain of human resources (HR).

1 Introduction

Understanding employees' preferences and opinions can be of paramount importance in the full employee life cycle, e.g., from recruitment and selection to employee retention, and performance and career management (Bogers et al., 2022). In employee satisfaction surveys, open-ended questions may elicit a wide range of aspects. However, conducting large-scale analysis of these responses is challenging because of their user-generated nature.

Aspect-based sentiment analysis (ABSA) is the task of identifying and extracting sentiments toward specific aspects from free text, allowing a more detailed analysis of opinions (Pontiki et al., 2016), which means they can be a valuable tool for identifying specific areas of (dis)satisfaction.

Despite the promise of ABSA, limited research has explored its application beyond English (Nazir et al., 2020). Moreover, to our knowledge, ABSA has not been studied in employee satisfaction surveys. This study aims to bridge this research gap by studying ABSA on Dutch open-ended employee satisfaction survey responses. The central research question that we answer in this paper is:

RQ1 *How effective is a BERT-based machine learning model in extracting aspect-sentiments from Dutch open-ended responses of employee satisfaction surveys?*

To answer this question, we first aim to answer the following sub-questions:

RQ1.1 *How does the performance of few-shot classification using Dutch BERT models compare to bag-of-words based baselines in ABSA?*

RQ1.2 *How does the performance of few-shot classification using Dutch BERT models compare to a zero-shot classification baseline in ABSA?*

RQ1.3 *To what extent can an improvement in performance be achieved in few-shot aspect-based sentiment classification, by training on a data set enlarged through data augmentation?*

Prior work mainly focuses on ABSA in English microblogs and user reviews. Microblogs, like X, cover diverse topics using informal language with an assumed shared context. Reviews tend to adopt more formal styles and primarily revolve around specific products or services (Kumar, 2019).

Open-ended survey responses share similarities with microblogs in terms of writing and context, but have topic coverage narrowed by topics that affect employee (dis)satisfaction.

[*]Work done while on internship at Randstad Groep Nederland

Proceedings of the First Workshop on Natural Language Processing for Human Resources (NLP4HR 2024), pages 16–26

This study compares the performance of Dutch pre-trained language models, BERTje (de Vries et al., 2019) and RobBERT (Delobelle et al., 2020), for ABSA in a few-shot classification experiment. These BERT-based models leverage contextual information, which is advantageous for short texts with limited contextual cues (Chang et al., 2020). We assess their performance against zero-shot classification BERTje and RobBERT models and traditional bag-of-words models (Wu, 2020).

The specific contributions of our research are as follows:

1. Annotation of a data set of 1,458 open-ended survey responses for ABSA in Randstad, with publicly available annotation procedures and guidelines for future studies.

2. Development of an ABSA model for Dutch open-ended employee satisfaction survey responses, enabling automated aspect-sentiment extraction for efficient and accurate analysis.

2 Related Work

This section provides an overview of previous studies on aspect and sentiment classification, ABSA, and the Dutch BERT models we employ in this paper: BERTje and RobBERT.

2.1 Aspect classification

Recent studies have found transformer models' effectiveness in topic and aspect classification on short text through their ability to capture long-range dependencies and context. Chang et al. (2020) demonstrated fine-tuning a deep transformer network for extreme multi-label aspect classification in English. In contrast, Dadgar et al. (2016) utilized a combination of TF-IDF vectors and an SVM classifier for news article aspect detection, without requiring extensive training. Hu et al. (2021) demonstrated few-shot learning using prototypical networks for aspect classification is valuable when labelled data is scarce. Alternatively, zero-shot classification, as discussed by Yin et al. (2019), allows topic classification without specific training, relying solely on labelled data for validation.

2.2 Sentiment classification

Sentiment classification is a long-standing research focus. Jiménez-Zafra et al. (2017) used an SVM classifier for patient satisfaction categorization in Dutch and Spanish healthcare reviews. Karl and Scherp (2022) demonstrated that larger transformer models, like RoBERTa, excel in sentiment classification over classic BERT models due to their ability to generalize to unseen data. These transformer models can also perform well in zero-shot multilingual sentiment classification, as shown by Tesfagergish et al. (2022). Dogra et al. (2021) illustrated the effectiveness of BERT-based models in few-shot sentiment classification. Between Dutch BERT models it was found that RobBERT outperforms BERTje in sentiment classification, credited to its enhanced training framework and a larger training corpus (De Bruyne et al., 2021).

2.3 Aspect-based sentiment analysis

Lin and He (2009) introduced joint aspect-sentiment analysis, combining LDA for aspect extraction and a polarity lexicon for sentiment classification in English movie reviews. However, Jiménez-Zafra et al. (2017) found this lexicon-based approach unsuitable for Dutch and Spanish.

ABSA gained prominence after SemEval-2014 task 4 (Pontiki et al., 2014), where researchers tackled identifying explicit terms or categories representing aspects of a target entity, and their polarities, in the context of restaurant and laptop reviews. Over time, the task expanded to encompass full and multilingual reviews.

De Clercq and Hoste (2016) attempted Dutch ABSA using SVMs, augmenting their bag-of-words (BoW) approach with semantic role labels, with limited success.

Recent advancements include Hoang et al. (2019) demonstrating the potential of BERT models in English ABSA, and Liao et al. (2021) improving performance with a RoBERTa-based model. Few-shot BERT classification and augmented training with BERT embeddings were explored by Hosseini-Asl et al. (2022). De Geyndt et al. (2022) employed a RobBERT model to extract features for SVM in ABSA, reporting better results than a full transformer-based approach for their pipeline.

ABSA in open-text survey responses was addressed by Cammel et al. (2020) and van Buchem et al. (2022) using techniques like LDA, rule-based methods, and non-negative matrix factorization with multilingual BERT. These studies primarily focused on patient survey questions in the healthcare domain. Additionally, Cammel et al. (2020) restricted to detecting a single aspect-sentiment per response, limiting broad insights. Both studies considered open-ended responses to different survey questions simultaneously, some of which elicited one-word responses which provided insufficient context for successful aspect-sentiment extraction.

2.4 Transformer models for Dutch

Transformers have excelled in Dutch aspect and sentiment classification, with two dedicated to Dutch: BERTje and RobBERT.

BERTje, with 12 layers, a hidden size of 768, and 12 attention heads, is pre-trained on a diverse corpus encompassing Wikipedia, news articles, books, and web pages, enabling it to capture Dutch linguistic patterns and context (de Vries et al., 2019). RobBERT, a Dutch variant of RoBERTa, shares a similar architecture with BERTje, but benefits from a more extensive pre-training dataset, including Wikipedia, news articles, web pages, Dutch parliament debates, and social media (Delobelle et al., 2020).

Existing methods for Dutch sentiment analysis are suboptimal, requiring further exploration, especially in novel domains like HR surveys.

3 Methodology

This section outlines the development and evaluation of the proposed ABSA model for Dutch open-ended survey responses on employee satisfaction.

3.1 Data set

The data set used in this study comprises Dutch open-ended responses to survey questions conducted by *anonymized*. We derived a sample of $1,500$ responses, recorded between January 2019 and December 2022, through stratified sampling across three different sub-brands of Randstad.

An example of such a response which illustrates the challenging nature of ABSA in employee satisfaction survey responses is: *"Ik ben tevreden over mijn salaris. Ik mis wel een stukje persoonlijke aandacht."* ("I am satisfied with my salary. However, I do miss some personal attention.") Here, we distinguish two aspect-sentiment pairs; an employee expresses a positive sentiment toward their salary, yet a negative sentiment toward personal attention. We explain the range of identified aspects in Section 3.3.

3.2 Data Preparation

We filtered and anonymized our set of responses to ensure data quality and privacy. We excluded responses with less than 10 tokens, as manual inspection revealed how shorter responses often lacked adequate contextual information for accurate aspect classification. We also excluded responses exceeding 512 characters to address computational constraints (Liao et al., 2021). The final average response length is 35.7 tokens (approximately 182 characters), with 10 tokens (39 characters) at a minimum, and 97 tokens (511 characters) at most.

To ensure anonymity of both respondents and individuals mentioned in responses, all personal information was removed and replaced by dummy variables by using the Dutch Named Entity Recognition (NER) SpaCy model and regular expressions. After identifying, we replaced person names with "Naam", email addresses with "Emailadres", and addresses with "Adres". After this, manual review corrected an additional 28 names missed by SpaCy.

3.3 Aspect selection

We preprocessed responses by retaining only nouns, proper nouns, and verbs because they convey the most informative content (Boguraev et al., 1999). We then applied lemmatization. Finally, we applied TF-IDF vectorization to represent each response. We then applied k-means clustering over these TF-IDF vectors, determining the optimal number of clusters at $k = 6$, using the elbow method.

We inspected the responses in each cluster. Table 1 shows the most important terms per cluster, indicated by the highest TF-IDF score. After analyzing these clusters, we found they roughly represent the aspects of *contact, salary, schedule, personal attention, communication,* and *agreements*. The cluster names were verified by two domain experts. We define each aspect below, accompanied by an illustrative example.

- **Contact**: refers to the extent to which an employee can get in touch with the agency, for example, by phone or email. - *It took a long time to receive a response from the contact person. I had to make multiple phone calls and send emails before getting a reply.*

- **Schedule**: is about scheduling, work hours, and days off and whether the agency is flexible in changing these. - *I appreciate receiving my schedule well in advance because it allows me to adjust my plans accordingly.*

- **Agreements**: relates to the arrangements made between the employee and the agency and whether these are upheld or not. - *I am* *satisfied with the schedule agreement because it allows me to take my kids to school.*

- **Salary**: is about payment and any bonuses or extras such as travel expenses. Consider remarks about correct payment of salary, and the frequency of salary payment. - *I am happy that I can choose my own frequency of payment.*
- **Personal attention**: is about the extent to which the agency pays personal attention to the employee. It can include receiving feedback and receiving personal guidance. - *I feel valued as an employee, and my ideas and suggestions are listened to attentively.*
- **Communication**: refers to the way information is exchanged between the agency and the employee, and whether communication about important matters is timely. - *I am satisfied with the way in which I am informed about the changes that are happening within the company.*

The *contact* and *communication* aspects may appear similar but are distinct: both revolve around interaction, but *contact* pertains to the accessibility and responsiveness between employees and the agency, emphasizing ease of access and availability. *Communication* is about information exchange, including factors like clarity, completeness, and timeliness.

3.4 Annotation Study

To collect labelled data, we ran an annotation study with nine native Dutch-speaking trainees from Yacht, which is one of the staffing agencies within Randstad. We had each response in the set of 1,500 responses annotated by three annotators, i.e., each annotator annotated 500 responses.

Annotators attended an in-person session to familiarize themselves with the task and guidelines. Detailed written guidelines, encompassing the task's objective, annotation procedure, answering options, and category definitions, were provided, along with examples for each category. To address annotator bias, a preliminary sample of 20 responses was annotated and discussed before each annotator worked on their assigned batch. We have published an English translation of our annotation guidelines online.[1]

[1] `https://anonymous.4open.science/r/AnnotationGuidelinesABSA-BB08/`

We employed the Prodigy annotation tool (Montani and Honnibal, 2018) with a custom recipe for annotation purposes. Annotators individually reviewed responses, selected relevant aspects, and a binary (positive or negative) sentiment for each aspect. They could also select 'no topics' if none of the six aspects were discussed. Responses were presented in random order to ensure unbiased judgment, and disagreements among annotators were resolved through majority voting, relying on a fourth annotator re-annotating in cases of no consensus.

Our primary focus was to identify clear-cut positive and negative sentiments for actionable insights on employee satisfaction. To address conflicting sentiments toward the same aspect, an 'ignore' option was introduced. Sentences marked with 'ignore' were excluded, enabling the model to focus on identifiable sentiment patterns. In addition, as sentiment was modeled as a binary variable, for neutral sentiments or multiple sentiments toward a single aspect, annotators used the 'ignore' option to ensure data consistency (Hartmann et al., 2023).

3.4.1 Inter-Annotator Agreement

Reliability in assessing inter-annotator agreement (IAA) is crucial. In this study, we employed Fleiss' kappa to measure agreement among multiple annotators, an extension of Cohen's kappa for more than two annotators (Fleiss, 1971).

With an average kappa score of 0.537, we achieved a moderate level of IAA, which reflects reliable annotations (Dumitrache et al., 2015) considering the inherent language ambiguity and inter-annotator disagreement.

The kappa statistic can be strict, especially in a multi-label setting, as it does not reward partial overlaps between annotations. Upon examining disagreement cases, we observed that when two out of three annotators agreed on the exact annotation, 53.92% of the responses exhibited a partial overlap between the majority-vote annotation and the third one. Additionally, 206 annotations (13%) required re-annotation by a fourth annotator due to three annotators providing different answers.

A quantitative analysis investigated disagreement patterns among aspects. Out of 106 responses with disagreement, a notable pattern emerged regarding the 'communication' aspect. In these cases, two annotators selected 'no topics,' while one chose 'communication:NEG.' This suggests a lack of clear demarcation in defining 'communication,' particularly in negative discussions. A similar pat-

Cluster	contact		salary		schedule		personal attention		communication		agreements	
	contact	contact	krijgen	to receive	week	week	mens	human	communicatie	communication	gesprek	conversation
	persoon	person	komen	to come	dag	day	contact	contact	verlopen	to go	horen	to hear
Top 5 terms	opnemen	to pick up	willlen	to want	uur	hour	krijgen	to receive	contact	contact	evaluatie	evaluation
	vraag	question	vragen	to ask	maand	month	nummer	number	komen	to come	bellen	to call
	contactpersoon	contact person	jaar	year	krijgen	to receive	maken	to make	super	super	sollicitatie	job interview

Table 1: Six identified aspects obtained through clustering responses, with the top five terms with highest TF-IDF scores.

tern was observed for 'personal attention,' possibly due to its over-representation in the dataset. Additionally, aspects with the highest agreement also generated substantial disagreement, likely because of their high frequency in the dataset. We found similar patterns for aspects with low occurrence.

In conclusion, the annotation study resulted in a dataset of 1,500 responses. Among these, 42 responses were categorized as 'ignore' due to conflicting or neutral sentiments and were excluded. After their removal, the final dataset comprised 1,458 responses, with 267 discussing aspects positively and 1,091 featuring negative discussions. See Table 2 for a detailed distribution of aspect and sentiment labels.

Label	POS_Count	NEG_Count	total
agreements	8	67	75
communication	33	212	245
contact	57	155	212
personal attention	141	370	511
schedule	5	134	139
salary	23	153	176
no topics	0	0	376
total	267	1091	1734

Table 2: Distribution of aspects and sentiments. POS_Count indicates the number of positive occurrences in the data set; NEG_Count indicates the negatives.

3.5 Data Augmentation

Table 2 reveals significant label imbalance in both aspects and sentiments, e.g., 'personal attention' is disproportionately represented, occurring nearly five times more than 'agreements'. In addition, the majority (approximately 78.77%) of aspects have a negative sentiment.

To address this imbalance and prevent bias in the machine learning model, data augmentation was implemented using NLPaug (Ma, 2019). This approach involves generating contextual word embeddings using a BERT model and replacing some of the tokens in a sentence (Sarhan et al., 2022). For an example of an original sentence and its augmented version: *"De lonen zouden wel een keer flink omhoog mogen"* ("the wages could well do with a substantial increase") is rephrased into *"De salarissen zullen tot twintig keer dik omhoog moeten."* Here, some tokens from the initial sentence were replaced with contextually analogous tokens to yield the augmented sentence. However, this carries the risk of creating ungrammatical augmented sentences, as in the example.

Data augmentation used RobBERT embeddings to increase label combination variety until each distinct label combination occurred at least 30 times. RobBERT was chosen for its wider training data set, enabling broader coverage of Dutch texts. Because the objective was to extract multiple aspect-sentiments from open-ended survey responses, augmentation focused on responses with two or more aspects. With a 30% set augmentation probability and a maximum of 50 tokens, data augmentation involved replacing up to 50 tokens in a response. The augmented responses were added to the training data set, as shown in Table 3, which displays the distribution of labels and sentiments across both the augmented and non-augmented training data set. Although Table 3 demonstrates the additional training samples improved balance, a slight imbalance remains.

	POS_Count		**NEG_Count**	
Label	original	augmented	original	augmented
agreements	6	200	43	516
communication	21	516	140	745
contact	28	432	111	803
personal attention	101	550	239	716
schedule	3	98	85	420
salary	13	380	102	539
total	172	2176	720	3739

Table 3: Aspect and sentiment distribution of the original versus the augmented training data set.

3.6 Model implementation

For aspect-based sentiment analysis of open-ended survey responses, we propose a two-tiered approach. The first step employs multi-label classification to determine the correct aspects for each response. The second utilizes the aspects identified by the first system as features, along with the response, and assigns binary sentiment labels to each aspect within the response. The adoption of a two-tiered approach serves a dual purpose. Firstly, it allows the model to concentrate exclusively on aspect identification in its initial step. This deliberate isolation permits the model to specialize in autonomously recognizing aspects before undertaking sentiment classification. Moreover, the two-tiered framework is strategically designed to mitigate challenges associated with data sparsity in the dataset. Given that certain aspects may possess limited training examples, a 12-class multilabel classification experiment could potentially yield inadequate representations for specific aspects. This limitation may compromise the model's capacity to generalize beyond the training data and perform optimally across the entire spectrum of aspect-sentiment classes.

3.6.1 Baselines

For aspect and sentiment classification we employ support vector machines (SVM), multilayer perceptron (MLP), and two Dutch BERT models (BERTje and RobBERT) in a zero-shot classification setting as baselines. We selected BERTje and RobBERT for their success in similar tasks, and the advantage of pre-training on a larger corpus of Dutch texts (Cammel et al., 2020; van Buchem et al., 2022; De Geyndt et al., 2022).

We apply hyperparameter tuning on a validation set, relying on a 70/15/15 train/test/validation split. For SVM, we found C=1000 and gamma=0.01 to be the optimal hyperparameters. For MLP, we found ReLU activation, Adam solver, and a hidden layer size of (256, 128) as optimal hyperparameters. For BERTje and RobBERT, we did parameter tuning on the training set, since no actual training was done. For aspect classification, each open-ended response was paired with all possible aspects, generating six inputs per response. Tokenisation was performed using the BERTje and RobBERT model tokenisers, following the guidelines provided by De Vries et al. (2019) and Delobelle et al. (2020). The network produced a probability vector of length six, indicating the likelihood of each aspect's presence in the response. Predicted class probabilities were initially notably below 0.5, perhaps due to the models' lack of training on the target domain data, so we tuned classification thresholds through a grid search, resulting in thresholds of 0.45 for BERTje and 0.37 for RobBERT. Maintaining a 0.5 threshold would have led to numerous false negatives.

For sentiment classification, we followed the same approach for SVM and MLP. For SVM we applied a linear kernel to fit the binary nature of the task. The optimal C parameter was found at 10. For MLP, we found ReLU activation, Adam solver, and a hidden layer size of (128, 64) to be optimal parameters. The preprocessed data was passed through the network, and the model output was a two-element vector representing positive and negative sentiment classes, with the sentiment having the highest value assigned as the predicted sentiment.

3.6.2 Aspect classification

In the aspect classification task, we fine-tune BERTje and RobBERT in a few-shot setting. To maintain consistent input length, batches of 16 tokenized samples were generated. The data set was randomly shuffled before training to mitigate order bias. The neural network consisted of a 12-layered BERT model with a dropout layer (dropout=.3) for regularization, and as output layer a linear layer with six dimensions representing six aspects. As both models converged around epoch 10 and to avoid overfitting, we stopped training at 10 epochs (Yu et al., 2019), using Adam optimizer with a learning rate of 0.005. Binary cross-entropy loss was calculated separately for each class with sigmoid activation and network weights were updated based on the total loss. This sigmoid activation approach allows for independent and interpretable probability estimates for the presence of each aspect, facilitating a comprehensive multilabel classification strategy.

3.6.3 Sentiment classification

For sentiment classification, BERTje and RobBERT were used in a few-shot classification setting. Input responses were padded, tokenized, and shuffled using a batch size of 4. Categorical aspect features were encoded using an embedding layer, and their embeddings were concatenated with the BERT embeddings of the responses to generate distinct sentiment predictions for each aspect.

The neural network for sentiment classification consisted of a 12-layer BERT model followed by a ReLU layer for learning complex patterns (Goodfellow et al., 2016), with a dropout layer (dropout=.3), followed by a 2 dimensional linear layer for the binary sentiment labels.

The model's performance was evaluated using cross-entropy loss after each iteration. A training function trained the model for 10 epochs with a learning rate of 0.005 using the Adam optimizer. For RobBERT's an BERTje's training loss and accuracy, we found they stabilized after the fourth epoch. However, we extended training to avoid premature stopping and underfitting (Yu et al., 2019). The loss continued to decrease until epoch 10, indicating no overfitting through extended training.

3.7 Evaluation Metrics

To evaluate aspect and sentiment classification tasks, we use the macro F1 score, which balances precision and recall and treats each category equally, mitigating the impact of larger classes. We also examine precision and recall to detect potential overfitting and underfitting as suggested by Sokolova and Lapalme (2009). The significance of the results is assessed using the Wilcoxon signed-rank test for aspect classification and McNemar's test for sentiment classification.

4 Results

In this section, we present the results of the experiments. We compare performance of BERTje$_{fewshot}$ and RobBERT$_{fewshot}$ to our traditional baselines (SVM and MLP), and zero-shot BERT baselines (BERTje$_{zeroshot}$ and RobBERT$_{zeroshot}$). In addition, we apply data augmentation for both (BERTje$_{fewshotDA}$ and RobBERT$_{fewshotDA}$).

4.1 Aspect classification

First, we turn to Table 4, which shows the performance of BERTje$_{zeroshot}$ and RobBERT$_{zeroshot}$. We note that, with 0.8793 recall and 0.1682 precision for RobBERT$_{zeroshot}$, and 0.9129 recall and 0.1568 precision for BERTje$_{zeroshot}$, both approaches show overprediction, which persists across all aspect categories.

The zero-shot models struggled to establish a reliable decision boundary for classifying aspects, indicating ineffective transfer of pre-training knowledge to novel data. The Dutch BERT models lacked domain-specific knowledge, aligning with prior findings for microblog texts (Chen et al., 2021).

Next, we compare the F1 scores of few-shot methods to all others, in Table 5. We see how BERTje$_{fewshot}$ and RobBERT$_{fewshot}$ at 0.5219 and 0.5449 respectively, significantly outperform all baselines ($p < 0.0001$). Between them, RobBERT$_{fewshot}$ significantly outperforms BERTje$_{fewshot}$ ($p < 0.0001$).

	precision		**recall**		**f1-score**	
	BERTje	RobBERT	BERTje	RobBERT	BERTje	RobBERT
agreements	0.0488	0.0784	1	0.9153	0.0928	0.1381
communication	0.1648	0.1623	0.9875	0.8441	0.2883	0.2662
contact	0.1478	0.1728	0.8394	0.8871	0.2575	0.2818
personal attention	0.3452	0.03591	0.892	0.8974	0.5084	0.513
schedule	0.0972	0.1072	0.8871	0.9167	0.1702	0.1983
salary	0.1283	0.1211	0.8954	0.8218	0.2148	0.2148
macro avg	0.1568	0.1682	0.9129	0.8793	0.2571	0.2671

Table 4: zero-shot aspect classification scores.

Our BoW baselines outperform the transformer-based zero-shot baselines, which suggest that the individual words captured by BoW models have a strong correlation with the aspects, and the contextual knowledge from BERT models may not offer sufficient information for distinguishing between aspects in open-ended survey responses.

We applied data augmentation to address label imbalance. BERTje$_{fewshotDA}$ achieves a lower F1 score (0.4982) than BERTje$_{fewshot}$ (0.5219), which suggests potential overfitting, or that the model gained limited novel information from augmented examples. However, RobBERT$_{fewshotDA}$ outperforms RobBERT$_{fewshot}$ with a significant increase in F1 score from 0.5449 to 0.6074 ($p = 0.017$). The performance improvement was particularly prominent in the 'agreements' category, which was underrepresented before augmentation. Nevertheless, data augmentation leads to decreased performance in some aspects.

Both zero-shot models suffer from overprediction, evidenced by high recall and low precision. This could be caused by a lack of knowledge from the target domain. This finding is supported by the outcomes of the few-shot classification experiment, where the significantly improved performance shows the model's improved capability to differentiate between the different aspect-classes, resulting in a higher macro F1 score. This illustrates the importance and benefits of fine-tuning, even when only a small amount of labelled target domain data is available.

4.2 Sentiment classification

Turning to sentiment classification results in Table 6, we see how BERTje$_{fewshot}$ with an F1 score of 0.8736 does not significantly outperform RobBERT$_{fewshot}$ at 0.8871 ($p = 0.292$). Both significantly outperform all baselines (all $p < 0.0001$). Again, BoW models outperform zero-shot models that seem to struggle to transfer contextual knowledge to the novel domain.

There seems to be no beneficial impact of data

	SVM	MLP	BERTje *zeroshot*	RobBERT *zeroshot*	BERTje *fewshot*	BERTje *fewshotDA*	RobBERT *fewshot*	RobBERT *fewshotDA*
agreements	0.2963	0.2222	0.0928	0.1356	0.2849	0.2871	0.1553	**0.4765**
communication	0.2857	0.1924	0.2883	0.2716	0.437	0.4298	0.3938	**0.4691**
contact	0.3619	0.4143	0.2575	0.2841	0.56	**0.5984**	0.5758	0.5546
personal attention	0.6025	0.5871	0.5084	0.5148	0.6324	0.7064	**0.7593**	0.6587
schedule	0.4	0.3238	0.1702	0.2019	0.4892	0.3581	0.6129	**0.7489**
salary	0.5227	0.4498	0.2148	0.2142	0.7329	0.6157	**0.7581**	0.6487
macro average	0.4115	0.3633	0.2571	0.2671	0.5219	0.4982	0.5449	**0.6074**

Table 5: Aspect classification performance in terms of F1 score for; best performing methods are boldfaced.

	SVM	MLP	BERTje *zeroshot*	RobBERT *zershot*	BERTje *fewshot*	BERTje *fewshotDA*	RobBERT *fewshot*	RobBERT *fewshotDA*
negative	0.9124	0.9024	0.2619	0.2938	0.9472	0.9423	**0.9576**	0.9482
positive	0.6228	0.5135	0.3348	0.3171	0.8	0.7912	**0.8314**	0.8186
macro average	0.7676	0.708	0.2983	0.3061	0.8736	0.8651	**0.8871**	0.8846

Table 6: Sentiment classification performance in terms of F1 score; best performing methods are boldfaced.

augmentation on sentiment classification, with neither BERTje$_{fewshotDA}$ nor RobBERT$_{fewshotDA}$ being able to outperform BERTje$_{fewshot}$ (0.8736 vs. 0.8651) and RobBERT$_{fewshot}$ (0.8871 vs. 0.8846).

5 Discussion

This study explores ABSA in Dutch employee satisfaction surveys, using Dutch BERT-based machine learning models. Our findings are in line with findings in prior research (Chang et al., 2020; Karl and Scherp, 2022) that highlight BERT's effectiveness for ABSA in English. Consistent with Karl and Scherp (2022), RobBERT outperforms BERTje, indicating the superiority of larger transformer models for sentiment classification, also observed by De Bruyne et al. (2021).

Additionally, our study underscores the success of few-shot classification in addressing limited labelled data, consistent with Hu et al. (2021) for aspect classification and Dogra et al. (2021) for sentiment classification in English. However, our findings contradict successful application of BERT models for zero-shot classification by Yin et al. (2019). This discrepancy in performance can be attributed to our domain-specific data, in contrast to the diverse dataset used by Yin et al. (2019).

Furthermore, this study identified significant label imbalance in aspects and their associated sentiments, as detailed in Section 4. To address this, we explored data augmentation using NLPaug (Ma, 2019) following Sarhan et al. (2022). However, this technique improved the macro F1 score for RobBERT in aspect classification only.

5.1 Limitations

Our dataset, comprising 1,458 responses, is relatively small which may affect its reliability. Despite time constraints, three annotators assessed each response for inter-annotator agreement. However, using larger and more diverse datasets can improve findings in future studies.

Using k-means clustering for aspect identification presents inherent limitations for internal and external validity. A substantial number of responses (376) didn't align with identified aspects, raising concerns about their reliability and comprehensiveness. Clustering does not support responses' potential membership of multiple clusters. Fuzzy clustering, as suggested by Zhao and Mao (2017), allows responses to belong to multiple clusters with varying membership degrees, offering a more comprehensive solution, at the cost of hindering clear boundaries and optimal cluster determination through the elbow method. Finally, using a supervised classification approach on an internal dataset provides accurate clustering results but reduces findings' transferability to emerging aspects, impacting external validity. Unsupervised clustering, as demonstrated by Cammel et al. (2020), may provide flexibility and adaptability to evolving contexts and domains.

To ensure high performance on future open-ended responses, further fine-tuning or retraining of the model with recent and relevant data is necessary.

6 Conclusion

Analyzing workforce opinions and preferences through aspect-based sentiment analysis has various HR applications. In this paper, we demonstrate the effectiveness of Dutch BERT models, BERTje and RobBERT, in a few-shot ABSA experiment using Dutch open-ended responses from employee satisfaction surveys. We address three sub-questions to gain insights into the models' performance and potential enhancements for aspect-based sentiment analysis (ABSA).

Regarding the first two sub-questions (RQ1.1 and RQ1.2), few-shot transformer models outperform baseline BoW models, significantly improving aspect-sentiment classification measured by macro F1 score. This emphasizes the importance of labeled data for fine-tuning BERT models, enhancing performance compared to relying solely on pre-trained knowledge in zero-shot scenarios. It also highlights BoW models' superior performance in leveraging individual words compared to zero-shot models struggling with domain transfer.

Regarding the third sub-research question (RQ1.3), this study demonstrates how data augmentation can enhance RobBERT's aspect classification performance. However, data augmentation does not improve aspect or sentiment classification for BERTje or sentiment classification for RobBERT. These findings suggest that the effectiveness of data augmentation varies across models and tasks.

In summary, regarding the main research question (RQ1) on BERT-based models' effectiveness in extracting aspect-sentiments, our findings demonstrate their superiority over traditional bag-of-words models and zero-shot classification approaches. To enhance model robustness, future studies should acquire larger and more diverse ABSA datasets, exposing models to varied open-ended survey responses for improved generalization to novel data. Considering the challenges posed by the limitations of traditional clustering methods, future studies could explore the incorporation of other clustering methods such as fuzzy clustering (Zhao and Mao, 2017) or semi-supervised (neural) topic modeling approaches (Chiu et al., 2022; Xu et al., 2023). Moreover, future studies should investigate the disparity in data augmentation success between BERTje and RobBERT. Specifically, exploring whether generating augmented sentences using BERTje embeddings improves BERTje model performance, similar to the favorable outcome observed for RobBERT in this study. Understanding such disparities would contribute to a deeper understanding of the relationship between specific models, their embeddings, and the efficiency of data augmentation techniques in ABSA's broader context.

Acknowledgements

The authors would like to thank PP for extensive infrastructural support in running our annotation study.

References

Toine Bogers, David Graus, Mesut Kaya, Francisco Gutiérrez, Sepideh Mesbah, and Chris Johnson. 2022. Second workshop on recommender systems for human resources (recsys in hr 2022). In *Proceedings of the 16th ACM Conference on Recommender Systems*, RecSys '22, page 671–674, New York, NY, USA. Association for Computing Machinery.

Branimir Boguraev, Rachel Bellamy, and Christopher Kennedy. 1999. Dynamic presentation of phrasally-based document abstractions. In *Proceedings of the 32nd Annual Hawaii International Conference on Systems Sciences. 1999. HICSS-32. Abstracts and CD-ROM of Full Papers*, pages 10–pp. IEEE.

Simone A Cammel, Marit S De Vos, Daphne van Soest, Kristina M Hettne, Fred Boer, Ewout W Steyerberg, and Hileen Boosman. 2020. How to automatically turn patient experience free-text responses into actionable insights: a natural language programming (nlp) approach. *BMC medical informatics and decision making*, 20(1):1–10.

Wei-Cheng Chang, Hsiang-Fu Yu, Kai Zhong, Yiming Yang, and Inderjit S Dhillon. 2020. Taming pretrained transformers for extreme multi-label text classification. In *Proceedings of the 26th ACM SIGKDD international conference on knowledge discovery & data mining*, pages 3163–3171.

Qi Chen, Wei Wang, Kaizhu Huang, and Frans Coenen. 2021. Zero-shot text classification via knowledge graph embedding for social media data. *IEEE Internet of Things Journal*, 9(12):9205–9213.

Jeffrey Chiu, Rajat Mittal, Neehal Tumma, Abhishek Sharma, and Finale Doshi-Velez. 2022. A joint learning approach for semi-supervised neural topic modeling. In *Proceedings of the Sixth Workshop on Structured Prediction for NLP*, pages 40–51, Dublin, Ireland. Association for Computational Linguistics.

Seyyed Mohammad Hossein Dadgar, Mohammad Shirzad Araghi, and Morteza Mastery Farahani. 2016. A novel text mining approach based on tf-idf and support vector machine for news classification.

In *2016 IEEE International Conference on Engineering and Technology (ICETECH)*, pages 112–116. IEEE.

Luna De Bruyne, Orphée De Clercq, and Véronique Hoste. 2021. Emotional robbert and insensitive bertje: combining transformers and affect lexica for dutch emotion detection. In *Workshop on Computational Approaches to Subjectivity and Sentiment Analysis (WASSA), held in conjunction with EACL 2021*, pages 257–263. Association for Computational Linguistics.

Orphée De Clercq and Véronique Hoste. 2016. Rude waiter but mouthwatering pastries! an exploratory study into dutch aspect-based sentiment analysis. In *Proceedings of the Tenth International Conference on Language Resources and Evaluation (LREC'16)*, pages 2910–2917.

Ellen De Geyndt, Orphée De Clercq, Cynthia Van Hee, Els Lefever, Pranaydeep Singh, Olivier Parent, and Veronique Hoste. 2022. Sentemo: A multilingual adaptive platform for aspect-based sentiment and emotion analysis. In *12th Workshop on Computational Approaches to Subjectivity, Sentiment & Social Media Analysis, collocated with ACL 2022*, pages 51–61. Association for Computational Linguistics.

Wietse de Vries, Andreas van Cranenburgh, Arianna Bisazza, Tommaso Caselli, Gertjan van Noord, and Malvina Nissim. 2019. BERTje: A Dutch BERT Model. arXiv:1912.09582.

Wietse De Vries, Andreas van Cranenburgh, Arianna Bisazza, Tommaso Caselli, Gertjan van Noord, and Malvina Nissim. 2019. Bertje: A dutch bert model. *arXiv preprint arXiv:1912.09582*.

Pieter Delobelle, Thomas Winters, and Bettina Berendt. 2020. Robbert: a dutch roberta-based language model. *arXiv preprint arXiv:2001.06286*.

Varun Dogra, Aman Singh, Sahil Verma, Kavita, NZ Jhanjhi, and MN Talib. 2021. Analyzing distilbert for sentiment classification of banking financial news. In *Intelligent Computing and Innovation on Data Science: Proceedings of ICTIDS 2021*, pages 501–510. Springer.

Anca Dumitrache, Lora Aroyo, and Chris Welty. 2015. Achieving expert-level annotation quality with crowdtruth. In *Proc. of BDM2I Workshop, ISWC*.

Joseph L Fleiss. 1971. Measuring nominal scale agreement among many raters. *Psychological bulletin*, 76(5):378.

Ian Goodfellow, Yoshua Bengio, and Aaron Courville. 2016. *Deep learning*. MIT press.

Jochen Hartmann, Mark Heitmann, Christian Siebert, and Christina Schamp. 2023. More than a feeling: Accuracy and application of sentiment analysis. *International Journal of Research in Marketing*, 40(1):75–87.

Mickel Hoang, Oskar Alija Bihorac, and Jacobo Rouces. 2019. Aspect-based sentiment analysis using bert. In *Proceedings of the 22nd nordic conference on computational linguistics*, pages 187–196.

Ehsan Hosseini-Asl, Wenhao Liu, and Caiming Xiong. 2022. A generative language model for few-shot aspect-based sentiment analysis. *arXiv preprint arXiv:2204.05356*.

Mengting Hu, Shiwan Zhao, Honglei Guo, Chao Xue, Hang Gao, Tiegang Gao, Renhong Cheng, and Zhong Su. 2021. Multi-label few-shot learning for aspect category detection. *arXiv preprint arXiv:2105.14174*.

Salud María Jiménez-Zafra, M Teresa Martín-Valdivia, Isa Maks, and Rubén Izquierdo. 2017. Analysis of patient satisfaction in dutch and spanish online reviews. *Procesamiento del Lenguaje Natural*, 58:101–108.

Fabian Karl and Ansgar Scherp. 2022. Transformers are short text classifiers: A study of inductive short text classifiers on benchmarks and real-world datasets. *arXiv preprint arXiv:2211.16878*.

H. Kumar. 2019. Sentiment analysis on imdb movie reviews using hybrid feature extraction method. *Int. J. Interact. Multim. Artif. Intell.*

Wenxiong Liao, Bi Zeng, Xiuwen Yin, and Pengfei Wei. 2021. An improved aspect-category sentiment analysis model for text sentiment analysis based on roberta. *Applied Intelligence*, 51:3522–3533.

Chenghua Lin and Yulan He. 2009. Joint sentiment/-topic model for sentiment analysis. In *Proceedings of the 18th ACM conference on Information and knowledge management*, pages 375–384.

Edward Ma. 2019. Nlp augmentation. https://github.com/makcedward/nlpaug.

Ines Montani and Matthew Honnibal. 2018. Prodigy: A new annotation tool for radically efficient machine teaching. *Artificial Intelligence*, to appear.

Ambreen Nazir, Yuan Rao, Lianwei Wu, and Ling Sun. 2020. Issues and challenges of aspect-based sentiment analysis: A comprehensive survey. *IEEE Transactions on Affective Computing*, 13(2):845–863.

Maria Pontiki, Dimitris Galanis, Haris Papageorgiou, Ion Androutsopoulos, Suresh Manandhar, Mohammed AL-Smadi, Mahmoud Al-Ayyoub, Yanyan Zhao, Bing Qin, Orphée De Clercq, et al. 2016. Semeval-2016 task 5: Aspect based sentiment analysis. In *ProWorkshop on Semantic Evaluation (SemEval-2016)*, pages 19–30. Association for Computational Linguistics.

Maria Pontiki, Haris Papageorgiou, Dimitrios Galanis, Ion Androutsopoulos, John Pavlopoulos, and Suresh Manandhar. 2014. Semeval-2014 task 4: Aspect based sentiment analysis. *SemEval 2014*, page 27.

Injy Sarhan, Pablo Mosteiro, and Marco Spruit. 2022. Uu-tax at semeval-2022 task 3: Improving the generalizability of language models for taxonomy classification through data augmentation. *arXiv preprint arXiv:2210.03378*.

Marina Sokolova and Guy Lapalme. 2009. A systematic analysis of performance measures for classification tasks. *Information processing & management*, 45(4):427–437.

Senait Gebremichael Tesfagergish, Jurgita Kapočiūtė-Dzikienė, and Robertas Damaševičius. 2022. Zero-shot emotion detection for semi-supervised sentiment analysis using sentence transformers and ensemble learning. *Applied Sciences*, 12(17):8662.

Marieke M van Buchem, Olaf M Neve, Ilse MJ Kant, Ewout W Steyerberg, Hileen Boosman, and Erik F Hensen. 2022. Analyzing patient experiences using natural language processing: development and validation of the artificial intelligence patient reported experience measure (ai-prem). *BMC Medical Informatics and Decision Making*, 22(1):1–11.

Jheng-Long Wu. 2020. Identifying emotion labels from psychiatric social texts using a bi-directional lstm-cnn model. *IEEE Access*.

Weijie Xu, Xiaoyu Jiang, Srinivasan Sengamedu Hanumantha Rao, Francis Iannacci, and Jinjin Zhao. 2023. vONTSS: vMF based semi-supervised neural topic modeling with optimal transport. In *Findings of the Association for Computational Linguistics: ACL 2023*, pages 4433–4457, Toronto, Canada. Association for Computational Linguistics.

Wenpeng Yin, Jamaal Hay, and Dan Roth. 2019. Benchmarking zero-shot text classification: Datasets, evaluation and entailment approach. *arXiv preprint arXiv:1909.00161*.

Fuxun Yu, Zhuwei Qin, Chenchen Liu, Liang Zhao, Yanzhi Wang, and Xiang Chen. 2019. Interpreting and evaluating neural network robustness. *arXiv preprint arXiv:1905.04270*.

Rui Zhao and Kezhi Mao. 2017. Fuzzy bag-of-words model for document representation. *IEEE transactions on fuzzy systems*, 26(2):794–804.

Rethinking Skill Extraction in the Job Market Domain using Large Language Models

Khanh Cao Nguyen[▲] **Mike Zhang**[ø]
Syrielle Montariol[▲] **Antoine Bosselut**[▲]
[▲]EPFL, Switzerland
[ø]IT University of Copenhagen, Denmark
syrielle.montariol@epfl.ch mikejj.zhang@gmail.com

Abstract

Skill Extraction involves identifying skills and qualifications mentioned in documents such as job postings and resumes. The task is commonly tackled by training supervised models using a sequence labeling approach with BIO tags. However, the reliance on manually annotated data limits the generalizability of such approaches. Moreover, the common BIO setting limits the ability of the models to capture complex skill patterns and handle ambiguous mentions. In this paper, we explore the use of in-context learning to overcome these challenges, on a benchmark of 6 uniformized skill extraction datasets. Our approach leverages the few-shot learning capabilities of large language models (LLMs) to identify and extract skills from sentences. We show that LLMs, despite not being on par with traditional supervised models in terms of performance, can better handle syntactically complex skill mentions in skill extraction tasks.[1]

1 Introduction

Skill Extraction (SE) is a challenging task in the job market domain that involves identifying and extracting specific skills mentioned in job postings, resumes, and other job-related documents. SE plays a crucial role in various job market applications, such as matching job seekers with relevant job opportunities or analyzing trends in the job market. Prior approaches to SE rely on rule-based methods or keyword-matching techniques (Khaouja et al., 2021; Ternikov, 2022). More recent methods, which are considered state-of-the-art, propose to fine-tune language models to solve the task (Zhang et al., 2022a, 2023). However, they heavily rely on manually annotated data, which is prohibitively expensive to collect, especially in this application that requires human resource domain experts.

In this paper, we investigate the use of large language models (LLMs) for SE in the job market domain. LLMs have been trained on massive amounts of text data and have shown great potential in capturing the underlying patterns and semantics of language. The SE task can be linked with the more generic entity recognition task in natural language processing (NLP). Named Entity Recognition (NER) is a widely studied task in NLP that involves identifying and classifying named entities in text. The typical approach to the NER problem is to formulate it as a sequence labeling task that assigns each token to a predefined entity-related label. Recent methods have attempted to tackle this task using LLMs, with limited success (e.g., Wang et al., 2023a; Ma et al., 2023).

First, we propose a review of the datasets for SE. We uniformize them and release them as a benchmark for future research in the field. It includes six publicly available datasets covering 4 languages (English, French, German and Danish) and various domains and skills categories: SAYFULLINA (Sayfullina et al., 2018), SKILLSPAN (Zhang et al., 2022a), GREEN (Green et al., 2022), GNEHM (Gnehm et al., 2022a), KOMPETENCER (Zhang et al., 2022b) and FIJO (Beauchemin et al., 2022).

We test the ability of LLMs to solve the tasks on these six datasets using various prompting techniques. We compare two types of task formulations, highlighting their impact on various aspects of the model's behavior. Through diagnosing the performance of LLMs, we identify a taxonomy of errors, quantifying their frequency and supporting it with descriptive statistics on the datasets and the model's predictions, comprising multiple skill mentions that are conjoined together. For example, a job posting might require "ability to develop reporting software and statistical softwares". In this case, the phrase "develop reporting software and statistical softwares" represents a conjoined skill, where

[1]Code is available at https://github.com/epfl-nlp/SCESC-LLM-skill-extraction and data at https://huggingface.co/datasets/jjzha

Proceedings of the First Workshop on Natural Language Processing for Human Resources (NLP4HR 2024), pages 27–42
March 22, 2024

multiple skills are combined together. However, the current BIO annotation scheme does not capture such complex skill mentions effectively, leading to difficulties in accurately extracting each skill. Following this, in our error analysis, we highlight LLM behavior that is seen as detrimental using common NER evaluation and annotation schemes, but may be more adapted to real-world settings.

2 Related Work

2.1 Skill Extraction

Recently, there has been an increase of interest in the task of SE. The general dynamic nature of labor markets has led to an increase in tasks related to job descriptions (JD), including SE (Kivimäki et al., 2013; Zhao et al., 2015; Sayfullina et al., 2018; Bhola et al., 2020; Gugnani and Misra, 2020; Fareri et al., 2021; Konstantinidis et al., 2022; Ao et al., 2023; Zhang et al., 2023). Some works define a more granular label space such as Zhang et al. (2022a). Here, they distinguish between skill and knowledge components. In Sayfullina et al. (2018), they only extract soft skills. Then, in Green et al. (2022), they tag for both hard and soft skills. For other languages, in Gnehm et al. (2022b), they classify for only ICT-based skills in German. Last, for Beauchemin et al. (2022), they tag for only soft skills in French.

All these works employ methods such as sequence labeling (Sayfullina et al., 2018; Smith et al., 2019; Chernova, 2020; Zhang et al., 2022a,c), multi-label classification on the document-level (Bhola et al., 2020), and graph-based methods (Shi et al., 2020; Goyal et al., 2023). Recent methodologies include domain-specific models where LMs are continuously pre-trained on unlabeled JD (Zhang et al., 2022a; Gnehm et al., 2022b). However, to the best of our knowledge, no work has applied LLMs to the task of SE in the job market domain. We use several datasets from previous work in Section 3.

2.2 Entity Recognition using LLMs

With the recent advances in large-scale pre-training, LLMs were able to capture rich contextual information and achieve impressive performance in various downstream tasks (OpenAI, 2023; Touvron et al., 2023). However, their performance in NER is still significantly below supervised baselines (Ma et al., 2023; Wang et al., 2023a). This is partly because, as a sequence labeling benchmark, NER requires a structured output from models. Meanwhile, the autoregressive nature of LLMs does not guarantee a uniform output representation. Jimenez Gutierrez et al. (2022) conducted a comprehensive study on entities and relation extraction using LLMs in the biomedical domain and concluded that contemporary techniques could not enable GPT-3 with in-context learning to surpass BERT-sized fine-tuned LMs. Ma et al. (2023) and Wang et al. (2023a) reach similar conclusions in the general domain. Wang et al. (2023b) proposed a method to surround entities with special tokens, bridging the gap between sequence labeling and generative tasks and achieving comparable results compared to state-of-the-art pre-trained models. In more recent works, PromptNER (Ashok and Lipton, 2023) provides the entity definition to the model, asking it to output a list of potential entities along with the reasoning on the compatibility of each entity with the provided definition. Meanwhile, UniversalNER (Zhou et al., 2023) instruction-tunes smaller scale open-source models for entity extraction tasks.

3 Datasets for Skill Extraction

We gather and uniformize six datasets with the B-I-O annotation scheme, where each word in a sentence is associated with one tag. The "B" tag indicates that the associated word marks the *Beginning* of a span; "I" indicates a word *Inside* a span, and "O" marks words *Outside* a span. Each dataset is extracted from job ads from various domains and languages, and some are augmented with fine-grained annotations. Despite the disparity of the train-dev-test split proportion, we kept the original splits from the authors of each dataset to ensure comparability with previously published results.

For each dataset, we describe how they were created, and their content. Table 1 provides information on their size, language, domain and labels. Table 2 presents descriptive statistics of the six datasets, such as average sentence length and number of skills.

FIJO (Beauchemin et al., 2022) [2] A French job ad dataset annotating skill types using a sequence labeling approach. The skill groups are based on the AQESSS public skills repositories and proprietary skill sets provided by their collaborators. These skill types are divided into four categories: "Thoughts", "Results", "Relational", and "Personal".

[2]https://huggingface.co/datasets/jjzha/fijo

Name	Train	Dev	Test	Language	Domain	Labels
GREEN	8,669	964	335	English	Multiple	Qualific., Domain, Occupation, Exp., Skills
SKILLSPAN	4,800	3,174	3,569	English	Multiple	Skills, Knowledge
SAYFULLINA	3,705	1,855	1,851	English	Multiple	Soft Skills
GNEHM	19,889	2,332	2,557	German	ICT	ICT
FIJO	399	49	49	French	Insurance	Thoughts, Results, Relational, Personal
KOMPETENCER	778	346	262	Danish	Multiple	Skills, Knowledge

Table 1: **Datasets Overview:** number of sentences in each split, language, the domain of the job ads, and which type of labels are originally present in the dataset.

Name	Avg. Sentence Length	Avg. # of Skills	% Sentence w/o Skills	Avg. Skills Span Length	Tot. Unique Skills
GREEN	22.94	2.0	30.45	2.68	610
SKILLSPAN	11.99	0.3	83.64	3.56	986
SAYFULLINA	14.35	1.0	0.1	1.75	581
GNEHM	10.77	0.3	82.82	1.32	675
FIJO	31.70	2.4	16.0	9.7	123
KOMPETENCER	13.16	0.4	83.2	3.79	103

Table 2: **Test Split Datasets Statistics:** Average sentence length (number of words), average number of labeled skills per sentence, percentage of sentences in the dataset without any skill, average number of words in a skill span, and total number of unique skills in the test set.

GNEHM (Gnehm et al., 2022a) [3] This is a Swiss-German job ad dataset focusing on Information and Communications Technology (ICT)-related sequence labeling. It includes ICT tasks, technology stack, responsibilities, and so forth. This dataset is a combination of two other Swiss datasets, the Swiss Job Market Monitor and an online job ad dataset (Gnehm and Clematide, 2020; Buchmann et al., 2022).

GREEN (Green et al., 2022) [4] This English dataset is a token-level sequence labeling task containing five types of tags: Skills, Qualifications, Domain, Experience, and Occupation labels. The JDs present in the dataset are from the United Kingdom. The industries represented in the data are from various fields, such as IT, finance, healthcare, and sales.

SAYFULLINA (Sayfullina et al., 2018) [5] This dataset, in English, focuses on soft skill prediction. Soft skills are personal qualities such as "team working", "being dynamic", and "independent".

SKILLSPAN (Zhang et al., 2022a) [6] This job posting dataset includes annotations for skills and knowledge, derived from the ESCO taxonomy. In a nutshell, *knowledge* are things that you can learn, and *skills* show how you apply this knowledge. The skills can be relatively long. The data is in English and contains JDs from Stackoverflow and a source that contains various other positions.

KOMPETENCER (Zhang et al., 2022b) [7] This dataset includes JDs in Danish. The annotation scheme is the same as SKILLSPAN.

4 Method

In this work, we formulate the task of skills extraction as a LLMs generation task, leveraging LLMs' emergent in-context learning ability. The LLM is provided instructions, a set of demonstrations, and a sample to annotate. The instructions define the expected output format precisely. This format is crucial for NER tasks, as the rigid structure of the annotations and metrics poses a challenge in evaluating the generative output. In the following section, we describe our approaches and strategies to design prompt formats.

4.1 Prompting Strategies

We investigate two prompting strategies: EXTRACTION-STYLE and NER-STYLE, illustrated in Figure 1.

EXTRACTION-STYLE The spans extracted from the sentences are directly generated as a list, as

[3] https://huggingface.co/datasets/jjzha/gnehm

[4] https://huggingface.co/datasets/jjzha/green

[5] https://huggingface.co/datasets/jjzha/sayfullina

[6] https://huggingface.co/datasets/jjzha/skillspan

[7] https://huggingface.co/datasets/jjzha/kompetencer

shown in Figure 1. The output format is generated from the BIO-tag annotations by extracting the skills and concatenating them with a separator (in this case, a "\n" token).

NER-STYLE Following (Wang et al., 2023a), we formulate the output format by rewriting the original sentence and adding special tokens around each entity. This leads to a more constrained output format, leaving less space for hallucination. In practice, we wrap every skill from the original sentence with special token "@@" and "##", as shown in Figure 1.

Dataset-Specific Prompt In the absence of supervision from a large train set, the model has no way of knowing what exactly are the entities it is asked to extract. We create dataset-specific prompts to guide it, highlighting key information about the input sentence (domain, language) and the targeted entities (type of skills). We follow a specific template:

```
You are given a sentence from a job
description in <LANGUAGE>, in the
<DOMAIN> domain. Extract all the
<SKILL TYPE> that are required from
the candidate, <PROMPT-SPECIFIC
OUTPUT>.
```

For example, for the GNEHM dataset with EXTRACTION-STYLE prompt, we have:

```
You are given a sentence from a job
advertisement in German. Extract
all the IT/Technology skills and
competencies that are required from
the candidate as a list.
```

4.2 Demonstration Selections

LLMs are sensitive to the different combinations of in-context examples (Liu et al., 2022; Wang et al., 2023c). We experiment with two strategies to select demonstrations.

Semi-random Demonstrations We randomly select k examples from the train set. Due to the noisiness of the data, we manually inspect the examples, excluding low-quality ones. This process is time-consuming for high values of k; however, in our setting, having a high number of demonstrations ($k > 5$) doesn't improve the extraction performance (see Figure 3 in Appendix).

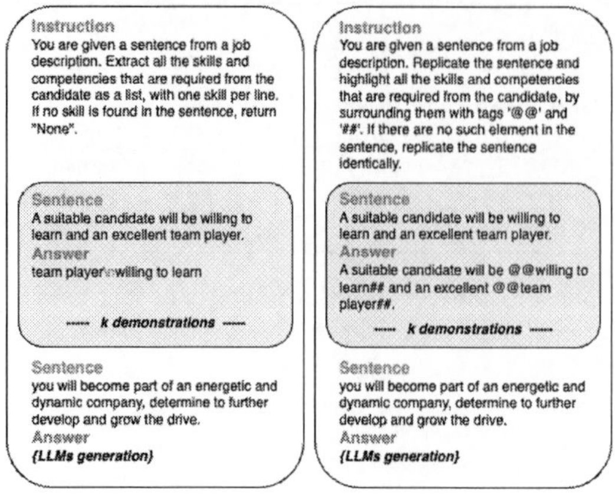

Figure 1: **Prompting Approaches.** EXTRACTION-STYLE **(left)**: The model extracts skills and presents them as a list, joined by a separator token; NER-STYLE **(right)**: The LLM rewrites the original sentence, with all skill mentions wrapped by special tokens "@@" and "##".

kNN-retrieval demonstrations To leverage demonstrations that are closely related to each sample, we use a kNN-retrieval approach. We embed each sentence using in-domain, monolingual masked language models (MLM), and retrieve the top k closest sentences in the train set using cosine similarity.

Mix of Positives and Negatives We define a ***negative*** demonstration as a sample from the training subset that does not contain any skill, and a ***positive*** one otherwise.

We create a mix of positive and negative demonstrations with a 1:1 ratio. When performing kNN-retrieval, we retrieve the nearest neighbors separately in the pools of positive and negative examples. Throughout our experiments, we denote k-shot a prompt with k positives and k negatives demonstrations.

4.3 Post-processing

Depending on the prompting strategies, we implement post-processing pipelines to extract the entities from the LLM's outputs. Indeed, since LLMs are trained for text generation instead of sequence labeling, they struggle with replicating spans of the input sequence as required for NER.

Even with in-context examples, LLMs fail to generate the required output correctly. In particular, on top of failing to respect the format (e.g., adding the right tags around entities for the NER-STYLE

PROMPTING), it often fails to correctly replicate the spans of the input sentence. Indeed, since the model generates the most probable sequence, it usually attempts to correct the errors found in the input sentence, such as spacing around punctuation or typos. Thus, in the process, it modifies the initial spans and prevents them from being accurately matched with the original input sentence, hindering the evaluation.

To address this issue, we propose a rule-based post-processing step that handles mismatched punctuation and minor edits made to the span by the model. We manually look at a sample of mismatches between LLM generations and original sentences and identify a set of common mismatches (see examples in Appendix C for categories and examples). We automatically detect if the model generation falls in one of these cases, and correct it using heuristics (e.g. added/removed spaces, punctuation insertion or deletion). Otherwise, we implement a feedback loop to prompt it to correct its answer. We feedback on the original prompt as well as the model's answer, describe the mistake it makes, and request another generation with the instructions below.

EXTRACTION-STYLE:

```
You have correctly extracted these skills: <CORRECTLY EXTRACTED SKILL>. The following skills you extracted are either absent or not written the same way as in the original sentence: <INCORRECTLY EXTRACTED SKILL>. Modify these skills to make sure to exactly replicate these skills from the input sentence with their original spellings and grammars, discard any of them if needed. Remember to keep the skills that you correctly extracted. Provide them with one skill per line.
```

NER-STYLE:

```
You didn't correctly replicate the given sentence. Make sure the sentence stays the same, even if there are no skills to highlight, including punctuation, spacing, and grammar mistakes. Don't add any extra words or punctuation to the sentence except for the ## and @@ tags. Don't add nor remove any space. Remember to keep the valid highlighted skills with tags '@@' and '##': <CORRECTLY EXTRACTED SKILL>
```

If one feedback loop is not enough, we repeat the process of providing feedback and requesting another generation up to 3 times. If the desired format is not achieved after 3 retries, we consider that the model failed to extract any entity. We perform an extensive analysis of failure cases in Section 5.3.

5 Experiments

5.1 Experimental Framework

Models We use GPT-3.5-turbo[8] for all of our experiments, which has an input context of 4096 tokens. We set the temperature to 0 to enforce deterministic generation from the model. We also experiment with GPT-4 to set an upper-bound expectation for the performance. Due to budget constraints, we evaluate GPT-4 on a subset of samples.

To retrieve demonstrations, we use monolingual pre-trained models adapted to each dataset language. If possible, we use models fine-tuned on domain-specific datasets: JobBERT[9] for English, DaJobBERT[10] for Danish, jobBERT-de[11] for German, and CamemBERT[12] for French. The latter is the only one which is not specifically fine-tuned on jobs postings.

Baselines As baselines, we use the supervised results from Zhang et al. (2023) which are currently state-of-the-art. The model is ESCOXLM-R, an XLM-R_{large}-based encoder model (Conneau et al.,

[8] gpt-3.5-turbo-instruct

[9] https://huggingface.co/jjzha/jobbert-base-cased

[10] https://huggingface.co/jjzha/dajobbert-base-uncased

[11] https://huggingface.co/agne/jobBERT-de

[12] https://huggingface.co/camembert-base

2020), further pre-trained using the ESCO taxonomy (le Vrang et al., 2014) by employing a combination two training objectives: Masked language modeling and a three-way classification of whether concepts in ESCO are in connection with each other, to adapt the model to the job market domain. The supervised results are from fine-tuning the model on the training set of each dataset separately.

Evaluation Metrics The metrics are Precision (**P**), Recall (**R**) and span-F1 (**F1**). We compute STRICT metrics using `seqeval`.[13] We implement a RELAX skill-level metric, in which we considered an extracted entity as correct even if it only ***partially overlaps*** with the gold span from the annotation. The RELAX metric aims to evaluate the ability of LLMs to localize the skills within the given sentence.

5.2 Experimental Results

Table 3 compare the two prompting styles with various demonstration retrieval settings: zero-shot, 5-shots (a mix of 5 randomly retrieved negative demonstrations[14] and 5 random positive demonstrations), and 5-shots+kNN (top 5 nearest neighbors retrieved from the set of negative examples, and top 5 positive examples). All examples are retrieved from the train set of the datasets. The choice of 10 demonstrations stems from an ablation study reported in Figure 3 in Appendix. In the zero-shot setting, we always use the dataset-specific prompts to guide the model toward the desired type of entities to extract. The full table with precision and recall can be found in appendix (Table 7).

There is a large drop in performance across most datasets compared to fine-tuning models, for both the EXTRACT and NER-STYLE approaches. Aside from FIJO, in which GPT-3.5 with in-context learning achieves a comparable performance, in all other datasets the decrease margin is significant, with up to 50% decreases in F1 metrics.

The datasets with the largest performance drop are GNEHM and SAYFULLINA. We hypothesize that pre-trained models achieve better performances when the length of span entities is rather short (Table 2). The RELAX metric shows much higher performance (up to 20% higher average F1 score). In particular the recall is considerably higher, showing that LLMs are able to localize the skills within a sentence, but fail to capture the exact sequence. Concisely, we have the following findings:

Few-shot demonstrations are critical to model performance, with an average improvement of 20.0% for EXTRACT-STYLE and 28% for NER-STYLE in F1 when providing 5-shot demonstrations. Indeed, given the strict structure required by NER, it is essential to show the model examples of the specific output format, especially for NER-STYLE format.

EXTRACT-STYLE outperforms NER-STYLE prompting on average, especially with the RELAX evaluation scheme, in contrast to the findings of Wang et al. (2023b).

kNN-retrieval outperforms random selection of demonstrations across all benchmarks except SKILLSPAN. On average, switching from random to kNN demonstrations slightly improves the precision but greatly improves the recall (4% increases for both EXTRACT-STYLE and NER-STYLE). **Dataset-specific prompts improve the performance** on average, particularly on datasets highly specialized toward a specific domain (insurance for FIJO, IT for GNEHM) or skill type (soft skills only for SAYFULLINA).

5.3 Error analysis

Failure cases related to instruction-following errors Despite our post-processing pipeline, the LLM output often drifts from the desired format. Table 4 shows the number of failure cases from different prompting strategies; a failure case happens when the LLM fails to output the desired format after 3 feedback loops. *Zero-shot* inference exhibits the largest number of failures across almost all experiments by a large margin, as the instructions are not detailed enough to cover all potential output format divergences by the LLM. Providing demonstrations drastically reduces the number of failure cases. However, using kNN-retrieval does not necessarily reduce it further, even increasing the failure rate for NER-STYLE.

Impact of various dataset features Figure 2 shows how several sample features affect the extraction performances of the LLM, for both prompting strategies. **The number of skills per sentence** does not greatly affect extraction capabilities, for both EXTRACTION-STYLE and NER-STYLE. The **Skill span length** (from 1 to 10 words) affects the

[13] `https://github.com/chakki-works/seqeval`

[14] Except for SAYFULLINA, where there are only 4 negative training samples.

STRICT	FIJO F1	GNEHM F1	KOMPE-TENCER F1	GREEN F1	SKILL-SPAN F1	SAYFUL-LINA F1	AVG P	AVG R	AVG F1
SUPERVISED	42.0	88.4	49.8	51.2	62.6	92.2	–	–	64.4
EXTRACT-STYLE									
zero-shot+*specific*	0.0	21.0	15.9	4.4	6.5	11.6	19.8	7.15	9.9
5-shot	28.7	27.5	21.6	24.2	**25.0**	29.3	23.3	35.5	26.1
+*kNN*	34.3	29.0	**22.4**	29.0	20.9	33.3	24.4	39.4	28.1
+*kNN*+*specific*	35.7	40.5	20.9	28.4	20.3	**39.0**	**26.6**	**41.1**	**30.8**
NER-STYLE									
zero-shot+*specific*	3.0	7.4	1.6	0.7	2.3	0.4	6.53	1.8	2.57
5-shot	33.3	33.1	20.4	28.7	17.8	27.0	23.8	35.5	26.7
+*kNN*	36.7	32.3	15.3	**32.0**	15.5	32.3	23.3	39.3	27.4
+*kNN*+*specific*	**44.2**	**40.9**	16.1	31.8	13.7	36.6	26.4	40.9	30.5
GPT-4*									
EXTRACT-STYLE	38.0	58.7	**25.3**	**30.6**	**27.8**	**40.5**	33.3	**44.1**	36.8
NER-STYLE	**48.0**	**67.8**	24.6	21.9	25.7	38.4	**35.8**	42.7	**37.7**
RELAX	F1	F1	F1	F1	F1	F1	P	R	F1
EXTRACT-STYLE									
5-shot	70.0	35.0	**46.3**	70.1	45.7	48.9	48.5	67.9	52.7
+*kNN*	80.3	35.6	45.9	**74.0**	**46.2**	50.6	49.1	73.7	55.4
+*kNN*+*specific*	78.8	47.8	44.8	73.6	45.4	**57.7**	**51.1**	**75.1**	**58.0**
NER-STYLE									
5-shot	57.4	28.9	37.0	64.1	32.6	47.6	41.8	59.9	44.6
+*kNN*	**82.0**	37.9	33.2	64.7	29.9	48.2	42.8	68.5	49.3
+*kNN*+*specific*	80.3	**48.2**	44.8	66.0	27.6	51.4	46.5	69.3	53.1

Table 3: **Results of Experiments**, measured using Precision (**P**), Recall (**R**) and span-F1 (**F1**) metrics. **GPT-4 results are based on a subset of* ≤ 350 *samples for each dataset.*

Strategies	EXTRACT-STYLE	NER-STYLE
zero-shot+*specific*	26.5162	12.8629
5-shot	3.4623	2.2982
+*kNN*	1.8105	3.1458
+*kNN*+*specific*	1.6867	1.9816

Table 4: Average percentage of samples for which the LLM failed to extract entities after 3 re-tries. Results are averaged across all datasets. The zero-shot setting gave the highest number of failures.

Prompt	Span Length	# Skills
NER	-2.10	+0.33
EXTRACT	-1.46	+0.31

Table 5: Difference between skills extracted by GPT-3.5 and gold annotations, for each prompting strategy. *Interpretation: GPT-3.5 extracts on average 0.3 more skills than the gold annotation.* We use kNN-5-shots with dataset-specific prompts. Full results per dataset can be found in Table 11 in Appendix.

performance: entities with short span length, typically 1-2 words, are more likely to be correctly extracted. F1 performance degrades as the span gets longer. Finally, the **sentence length** heavily affects NER-STYLE performance, which is considerably lower for short sentences (1-2 words) and gradually improves with longer ones. Meanwhile, EXTRACT-STYLE keeps a relatively stable performance across different sentence lengths.

General Behavior Table 5 showcases the flaws in the skills extraction task performed by GPT-3.5. Compared to the ground truth annotations, the LLM extracts shorter spans (on average over all datasets, 2.1 fewer words for NER prompting) and more skills (on average over all datasets, 0.33 more skills per sample for both prompting strategies). To diagnose the reasons for this discrepancy, we analyze a sample of errors.

5.4 Error taxonomy

We manually analyze 60 examples where LLMs made the wrong predictions, both with EXTRACT-

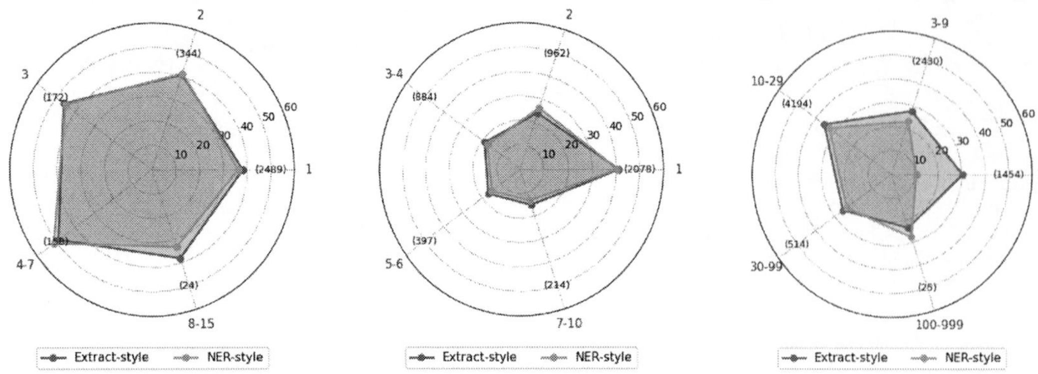

(a) *Number of skills* (b) *Skills span length* (c) *Sentence length*

Figure 2: **Analysis Statistics.** The F1 scores vary across different criteria. **(left)** Extraction performances across different numbers of skills in the sentence (excluding negative samples). **(middle)** Extraction performances for each bucket of lengths of skills span. **(right)** Extraction performances for different ranges of the sentences' length. We used the number of tokens as the measure of length. For simplicity, this error analysis was performed on the set of all datasets.

STYLE or NER-STYLE. The examples are randomly extracted with 10 from each dataset. Based on the analysis, we clustered the types of errors/misalignments between predictions and ground truths into different categories, listed below. Note that one sample can belong to several categories. We provide examples of each category in Appendix D (Table 10):

1. **Skill definition mis-alignment.** Misalignments between the definition of skills used by human annotators in the ground truth data, and what is considered a skill by the LLM. The errors are often career-related terminologies that are not exactly skills or competencies, but are still extracted by the LLM. This category accounted for up to ∼36% of the examined examples. We hypothesize that this category requires more demonstrations and more detailed instructions, potentially including definitions of skill types. The supervised model suffers much less from this flaw.

2. **Wrong extraction.** At times, the LLM also extracts spans that are completely unrelated to skills, competencies, or other career-related terminologies. 20% of samples fall into this category.

3. **Conjoined skills.** Here, we describe cases where a common span encompasses two skills. As an example, a job posting might require the "ability to develop reporting software and statistical software". The phrase "develop reporting software and statistical software" is a conjoined skill, where two skills (develop reporting software, and develop statistical software) are combined into a unique verb phrase. ∼14% of errors are attributed to this category. We approximate the true number of conjoined skills in the annotations for each dataset, using syntactic parsing. According to our measure, 16 to 22% of spans in 4 out of 6 datasets are conjoined skills. This observed behavior is in line with the metrics computed in Table 5 on differences between the LLM predictions and the ground truth annotations. Interestingly, we note that the prevailing BIO annotation scheme can not distinguish such skill mentions by construction, merging them into a unique span and yielding errors as well.

4. **Extended span.** ∼12% of the errors were instances where the LLM extracted longer spans than the ground truth, either by concatenating distinct skill mentions, or, more frequently, taking additional words around the gold skill mention.

5. **Incorrect annotations.** 8% of the errors were due to poor gold annotations. The annotated entity, while perhaps related to job markets, is irrelevant to skills, given the context.

6. **Other.** Other unidentified minor cases, such as LLM generations that do not conform to the expected format (∼10%). A common cause is

Dataset	% Conjoined skill
GREEN	21.87
SKILLSPAN	22.39
FIJO	17.79
SAYFULLINA	4.27
KOMPETENCER	16.67
GNEHM	0.02

Table 6: Proportion of entities that are conjoined skills in each dataset, obtained by performing syntactic parsing on the sentence.

the grammatical correctness of the input sentence, to which LLMs are extremely sensitive. In cases where the original sentence has an error, the LLM is attempting to correct it while solving the task. Consequently, when performing the evaluation, the generation from the model cannot be exactly matched with the original sentence.

6 Conclusion

In this paper, we benchmark and uniformize existing datasets for SE in job postings. We conduct in-depth experiments and error analysis to evaluate the ability of LLMs to solve the task, notably implementing two prompting strategies to adapt LLMs for the task and a dedicated feedback loop. In line with concurrent work (Han et al., 2023), LLMs achieve limited performance for skill extraction relative to supervised methods. Moreover, we highlight the limitations of the current SE task formulation and evaluation, focusing on the adaptation of the NER sequence labeling task, to the token generation task with which LLMs are pre-trained.

In particular, we list the causes of the most frequent errors in SE with GPT-3.5. In the absence of training data, LLMs struggle to understand what skills are and often extract irrelevant information. Additionally, GPT-3.5 tends to split conjoined skills into two, leading to less accurate but more granular skill extractions. In a real-world setting, in particular when SE is used as a preliminary step for skill classification in a taxonomy (e.g. ESCO, le Vrang et al., 2014), this behavior would be highly beneficial.

7 Limitations

Several limitations to this study should be considered.

Language. Despite our attempt to include as many datasets as possible, we are still limited in terms of language, as we include only four relatively high-resource languages: English, German, French, and Danish. This limits the generalizability of our findings to other languages, both in terms of the performance of LLMs and broader conclusions on the SE task.

Closed-source Models. Our analysis is done exclusively using closed-source models, gpt-3.5-turbo and gpt-4. We have little information on the data, architecture, and training processes of these models, which heavily limits our ability to interpret and justify their performance. Similarly, these models are updated regularly, limiting the reproducibility of these results.

Biases. Pre-trained language models suffer from the bias present in their training data and reflect it in their predictions. While state-of-the-art supervised models for SE are also pre-trained models (e.g. ESCOXLM-R (Zhang et al., 2023), fine-tuned from XLM-R), fine-tuning them on a high-quality, bias-controlled dataset for SE can mitigate the inherent bias present in the pre-training data (Wang and Russakovsky, 2023). Controlling the bias this way in LLMs such as GPT-3.5, when used in an in-context learning setting, is not an option and remains a challenging problem (Gallegos et al., 2023). Biased models, when implemented in the job market domain, can have serious downstream consequences on the hiring process of candidates, particularly with respect to under-represented communities.

Acknowledgements

We thank Jibril Frej (EPFL) for fruitful discussions and feedback on the first version of the paper. MZ is supported by the Independent Research Fund Denmark (DFF) grant 9131-00019B and in parts by ERC Consolidator Grant DIALECT 101043235. We also gratefully acknowledge the support of the Swiss National Science Foundation (No. 215390), Innosuisse (PFFS-21-29), the EPFL Science Seed Fund, the EPFL Center for Imaging, Sony Group Corporation, and the Allen Institute for AI.

References

Ziqiao Ao, Gergely Horváth, Chunyuan Sheng, Yifan Song, and Yutong Sun. 2023. Skill requirements in job advertisements: A comparison of skill-categorization methods based on wage regressions. *Information Processing & Management*, 60(2):103185.

Dhananjay Ashok and Zachary C. Lipton. 2023. Promptner: Prompting for named entity recognition. *CoRR*, abs/2305.15444.

David Beauchemin, Julien Laumonier, Yvan Le Ster, and Marouane Yassine. 2022. "FIJO": a French Insurance Soft Skill Detection Dataset. *Proceedings of the Canadian Conference on Artificial Intelligence*. Https://caiac.pubpub.org/pub/72bhunl6.

Akshay Bhola, Kishaloy Halder, Animesh Prasad, and Min-Yen Kan. 2020. Retrieving skills from job descriptions: A language model based extreme multi-label classification framework. In *Proceedings of the 28th International Conference on Computational Linguistics*, pages 5832–5842, Barcelona, Spain (Online). International Committee on Computational Linguistics.

Marlis Buchmann, Helen Buchs, Felix Busch, Simon Clematide, Ann-Sophie Gnehm, and Jan Müller. 2022. Swiss job market monitor: A rich source of demand-side micro data of the labour market. *European Sociological Review*.

Mariia Chernova. 2020. Occupational skills extraction with FinBERT. *Master's Thesis*.

Alexis Conneau, Kartikay Khandelwal, Naman Goyal, Vishrav Chaudhary, Guillaume Wenzek, Francisco Guzmán, Edouard Grave, Myle Ott, Luke Zettlemoyer, and Veselin Stoyanov. 2020. Unsupervised cross-lingual representation learning at scale. In *Proceedings of the 58th Annual Meeting of the Association for Computational Linguistics*, pages 8440–8451, Online. Association for Computational Linguistics.

Silvia Fareri, Nicola Melluso, Filippo Chiarello, and Gualtiero Fantoni. 2021. Skillner: Mining and mapping soft skills from any text. *Expert Systems with Applications*, 184:115544.

Isabel O Gallegos, Ryan A Rossi, Joe Barrow, Md Mehrab Tanjim, Sungchul Kim, Franck Dernoncourt, Tong Yu, Ruiyi Zhang, and Nesreen K Ahmed. 2023. Bias and fairness in large language models: A survey. *arXiv preprint arXiv:2309.00770*.

Ann-sophie Gnehm, Eva Bühlmann, Helen Buchs, and Simon Clematide. 2022a. Fine-grained extraction and classification of skill requirements in German-speaking job ads. In *Proceedings of the Fifth Workshop on Natural Language Processing and Computational Social Science (NLP+CSS)*, pages 14–24, Abu Dhabi, UAE. Association for Computational Linguistics.

Ann-Sophie Gnehm, Eva Bühlmann, and Simon Clematide. 2022b. Evaluation of transfer learning and domain adaptation for analyzing german-speaking job advertisements. In *Proceedings of the Language Resources and Evaluation Conference*, pages 3892–3901, Marseille, France. European Language Resources Association.

Ann-Sophie Gnehm and Simon Clematide. 2020. Text zoning and classification for job advertisements in German, French and English. In *Proceedings of the Fourth Workshop on Natural Language Processing and Computational Social Science*, pages 83–93, Online. Association for Computational Linguistics.

Nidhi Goyal, Jushaan Kalra, Charu Sharma, Raghava Mutharaju, Niharika Sachdeva, and Ponnurangam Kumaraguru. 2023. JobXMLC: EXtreme multi-label classification of job skills with graph neural networks. In *Findings of the Association for Computational Linguistics: EACL 2023*, pages 2181–2191, Dubrovnik, Croatia. Association for Computational Linguistics.

Thomas Green, Diana Maynard, and Chenghua Lin. 2022. Development of a benchmark corpus to support entity recognition in job descriptions. In *Proceedings of the Thirteenth Language Resources and Evaluation Conference*, pages 1201–1208, Marseille, France. European Language Resources Association.

Akshay Gugnani and Hemant Misra. 2020. Implicit skills extraction using document embedding and its use in job recommendation. In *The Thirty-Fourth AAAI Conference on Artificial Intelligence, AAAI 2020, The Thirty-Second Innovative Applications of Artificial Intelligence Conference, IAAI 2020, The Tenth AAAI Symposium on Educational Advances in Artificial Intelligence, EAAI 2020, New York, NY, USA, February 7-12, 2020*, pages 13286–13293. AAAI Press.

Ridong Han, Tao Peng, Chaohao Yang, Benyou Wang, Lu Liu, and Xiang Wan. 2023. Is information extraction solved by chatgpt? an analysis of performance, evaluation criteria, robustness and errors. *arXiv preprint arXiv:2305.14450*.

Bernal Jimenez Gutierrez, Nikolas McNeal, Clayton Washington, You Chen, Lang Li, Huan Sun, and Yu Su. 2022. Thinking about GPT-3 in-context learning for biomedical IE? think again. In *Findings of the Association for Computational Linguistics: EMNLP 2022*, pages 4497–4512, Abu Dhabi, United Arab Emirates. Association for Computational Linguistics.

Imane Khaouja, Ghita Mezzour, and Ismail Kassou. 2021. Unsupervised skill identification from job ads. In *2021 IEEE 22nd International Conference on Information Reuse and Integration for Data Science (IRI)*, pages 147–151. IEEE.

Ilkka Kivimäki, Alexander Panchenko, Adrien Dessy, Dries Verdegem, Pascal Francq, Hugues Bersini, and Marco Saerens. 2013. A graph-based approach to skill extraction from text. In *Proceedings of TextGraphs-8 Graph-based Methods for Natural Language Processing*, pages 79–87, Seattle, Washington, USA. Association for Computational Linguistics.

Ioannis Konstantinidis, Manolis Maragoudakis, Ioannis Magnisalis, Christos Berberidis, and Vassilios Peristeras. 2022. Knowledge-driven unsupervised skills extraction for graph-based talent matching. In *Proceedings of the 12th Hellenic Conference on Artificial Intelligence*, pages 1–7.

Martin le Vrang, Agis Papantoniou, Erika Pauwels, Pieter Fannes, Dominique Vandensteen, and Johan De Smedt. 2014. Esco: Boosting job matching in europe with semantic interoperability. *Computer*, 47(10):57–64.

Jiachang Liu, Dinghan Shen, Yizhe Zhang, Bill Dolan, Lawrence Carin, and Weizhu Chen. 2022. What makes good in-context examples for GPT-3? In *Proceedings of Deep Learning Inside Out (DeeLIO 2022): The 3rd Workshop on Knowledge Extraction and Integration for Deep Learning Architectures*, pages 100–114, Dublin, Ireland and Online. Association for Computational Linguistics.

Yubo Ma, Yixin Cao, YongChing Hong, and Aixin Sun. 2023. Large language model is not a good few-shot information extractor, but a good reranker for hard samples! *arXiv preprint arXiv:2303.08559*.

OpenAI. 2023. GPT-4 technical report. *CoRR*, abs/2303.08774.

Luiza Sayfullina, Eric Malmi, and Juho Kannala. 2018. Learning representations for soft skill matching. In *International Conference on Analysis of Images, Social Networks and Texts*, pages 141–152.

Baoxu Shi, Jaewon Yang, Feng Guo, and Qi He. 2020. Salience and market-aware skill extraction for job targeting. In *KDD '20: The 26th ACM SIGKDD Conference on Knowledge Discovery and Data Mining, Virtual Event, CA, USA, August 23-27, 2020*, pages 2871–2879. ACM.

Ellery Smith, Martin Braschler, Andreas Weiler, and Thomas Haberthuer. 2019. Syntax-based skill extractor for job advertisements. In *2019 6th Swiss Conference on Data Science (SDS)*, pages 80–81. IEEE.

Andrei Ternikov. 2022. Soft and hard skills identification: insights from it job advertisements in the cis region. *PeerJ Computer Science*, 8:e946.

Hugo Touvron, Louis Martin, Kevin Stone, Peter Albert, Amjad Almahairi, Yasmine Babaei, Nikolay Bashlykov, Soumya Batra, Prajjwal Bhargava, Shruti Bhosale, Dan Bikel, Lukas Blecher, Cristian Canton-Ferrer, Moya Chen, Guillem Cucurull, David Esiobu, Jude Fernandes, Jeremy Fu, Wenyin Fu, Brian Fuller, Cynthia Gao, Vedanuj Goswami, Naman Goyal, Anthony Hartshorn, Saghar Hosseini, Rui Hou, Hakan Inan, Marcin Kardas, Viktor Kerkez, Madian Khabsa, Isabel Kloumann, Artem Korenev, Punit Singh Koura, Marie-Anne Lachaux, Thibaut Lavril, Jenya Lee, Diana Liskovich, Yinghai Lu, Yuning Mao, Xavier Martinet, Todor Mihaylov, Pushkar Mishra, Igor Molybog, Yixin Nie, Andrew Poulton, Jeremy Reizenstein, Rashi Rungta, Kalyan Saladi, Alan Schelten, Ruan Silva, Eric Michael Smith, Ranjan Subramanian, Xiaoqing Ellen Tan, Binh Tang, Ross Taylor, Adina Williams, Jian Xiang Kuan, Puxin Xu, Zheng Yan, Iliyan Zarov, Yuchen Zhang, Angela Fan, Melanie Kambadur, Sharan Narang, Aurélien Rodriguez, Robert Stojnic, Sergey Edunov, and Thomas Scialom. 2023. Llama 2: Open foundation and fine-tuned chat models. *CoRR*, abs/2307.09288.

Angelina Wang and Olga Russakovsky. 2023. Overcoming bias in pretrained models by manipulating the finetuning dataset. *arXiv preprint arXiv:2303.06167*.

Shuhe Wang, Xiaofei Sun, Xiaoya Li, Rongbin Ouyang, Fei Wu, Tianwei Zhang, Jiwei Li, and Guoyin Wang. 2023a. Gpt-ner: Named entity recognition via large language models. *arXiv preprint arXiv:2304.10428*.

Shuhe Wang, Xiaofei Sun, Xiaoya Li, Rongbin Ouyang, Fei Wu, Tianwei Zhang, Jiwei Li, and Guoyin Wang. 2023b. GPT-NER: named entity recognition via large language models. *CoRR*, abs/2304.10428.

Xinyi Wang, Wanrong Zhu, and William Yang Wang. 2023c. Large language models are implicitly topic models: Explaining and finding good demonstrations for in-context learning. *arXiv preprint arXiv:2301.11916*.

Mike Zhang, Kristian Jensen, Sif Sonniks, and Barbara Plank. 2022a. SkillSpan: Hard and soft skill extraction from English job postings. In *Proceedings of the 2022 Conference of the North American Chapter of the Association for Computational Linguistics: Human Language Technologies*, pages 4962–4984, Seattle, United States. Association for Computational Linguistics.

Mike Zhang, Kristian Nørgaard Jensen, and Barbara Plank. 2022b. Kompetencer: Fine-grained skill classification in Danish job postings via distant supervision and transfer learning. In *Proceedings of the Thirteenth Language Resources and Evaluation Conference*, pages 436–447, Marseille, France. European Language Resources Association.

Mike Zhang, Kristian Nørgaard Jensen, Rob van der Goot, and Barbara Plank. 2022c. Skill extraction from job postings using weak supervision. In *Proceedings of RecSys in HR'22: The 2nd Workshop on Recommender Systems for Human Resources, in conjunction with the 16th ACM Conference on Recommender Systems*.

Mike Zhang, Rob van der Goot, and Barbara Plank. 2023. ESCOXLM-R: Multilingual taxonomy-driven pre-training for the job market domain. In *Proceedings of the 61st Annual Meeting of the Association for Computational Linguistics (Volume 1: Long Papers)*, pages 11871–11890, Toronto, Canada. Association for Computational Linguistics.

Meng Zhao, Faizan Javed, Ferosh Jacob, and Matt McNair. 2015. SKILL: A system for skill identification and normalization. In *Proceedings of the Twenty-Ninth AAAI Conference on Artificial Intelligence, January 25-30, 2015, Austin, Texas, USA*, pages 4012–4018. AAAI Press.

Wenxuan Zhou, Sheng Zhang, Yu Gu, Muhao Chen, and Hoifung Poon. 2023. Universalner: Targeted distillation from large language models for open named entity recognition. *arXiv preprint arXiv:2308.03279*.

A Additional Analysis

Main Results In addition to the F1 score, we also provide detailed results including the precision and recall for each prompting strategy, for both STRICT and RELAX metrics. Results are in Table 7.

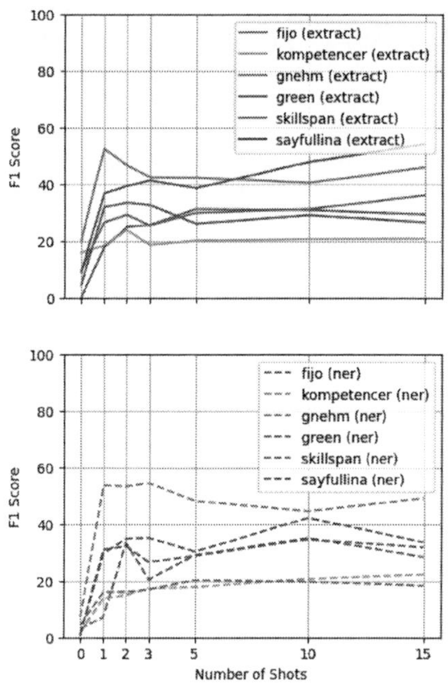

Figure 3: F1 performances of EXTRACT-STYLE and NER-STYLE on the full dataset of FIJO, KOMPETENCER, GREEN, and subset of 350 samples from GNEHM, SKILLSPAN, and SAYFULLINA. We recorded the experiments using $k = \{0, 1, 2, 3, 5, 10, 15\}$ shots. Demonstrations are retrieved randomly.

Impact of the number of demonstrations We conducted experiments to examine the impacts of the number of demonstrations k on the extraction results. Experiments are done on the full test set of FIJO, KOMPETENCER, GREEN, and a subset of 350 test samples for the other datasets to avoid an overhead in experimental cost. The result are recorded in Figure 4. Surprisingly, unlike the regarded knowledge that more demonstrations lead to better predictive capabilities, we only observed

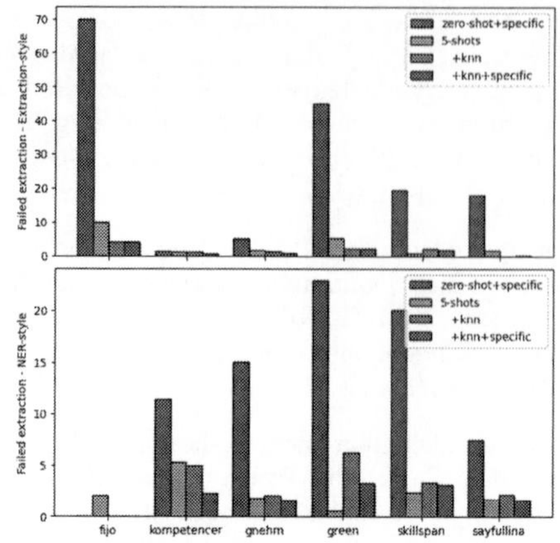

Figure 4: Percentage of samples in which LLM failed to extract entities after 3 re-tries. The zero-shot setting gave the most number of failures.

incremental performances for the first few demonstrations. After $k = 3$, we found that adding demonstrations did not guarantee better extraction results. Even for smaller k, certain datasets such as GNEHM also exhibited irregular performance patterns. We also found that increases are more stable for NER-STYLE approach, partially due to the highly structured and specific output format it requires.

Note that in our experiments, $k = i$ means that there are i positive and i negative examples in the demonstrations.

Failure cases Further breakdown of failure cases for each dataset can be found in Figure 4. In general, we found that the failure rates highly vary between datasets.

Impact of negative demonstrations Table 8 compares providing 10 positive examples as demonstrations with mixing 5 positive and 5 negative demonstrations. Experiments are done in a subset of ≤ 350 test samples with 5 shots.

For EXTRACT-STYLE prompting, providing positive-only demonstrations improves the F1 score for all datasets. Besides, positive-only context does not affect the frequency to which LLM predicts an example as negative (have **None** entities). On the other hand, the results vary for NER-STYLE. Notably, for this strategy, using positive-only demonstrations significantly abstains LLM from making negative predictions, with an average decrease of **None** samples of 44.9% and 29.1% for 3-shot and 5-shot, respectively. By allowing **None** predictions, a mixture of positives and negatives increases

STRICT	FIJO P	FIJO R	FIJO F1	GNEHM P	GNEHM R	GNEHM F1	KOMPETENCER P	KOMPETENCER R	KOMPETENCER F1	GREEN P	GREEN R	GREEN F1	SKILLSPAN P	SKILLSPAN R	SKILLSPAN F1	SAYFULLINA P	SAYFULLINA R	SAYFULLINA F1	AVG F1
SUPERVISED	–	–	42.0	–	–	88.4	–	–	49.8	–	–	51.2	–	–	62.6	–	–	92.2	64.4
EXTRACT-STYLE																			
zero-shot+*specific*	0.0	0.0	0.0	60.8	12.7	21.0	16.7	15.2	15.9	17.9	2.5	4.4	9.4	4.9	6.5	24.0	7.6	11.6	9.9
5-shot	29.8	27.6	28.7	18.3	55.1	27.5	14.8	**40.0**	21.6	26.3	22.5	24.2	**18.6**	**38.2**	**25.0**	29.2	29.5	29.3	26.1
+*kNN*	35.3	33.3	34.3	19.0	61.8	29.0	**16.2**	36.2	**22.4**	29.0	29.0	29.0	15.0	34.6	20.9	27.8	41.6	33.3	28.2
+*kNN+specific*	36.4	35.0	35.7	29.6	64.3	40.5	15.4	32.4	20.9	28.0	28.7	28.4	14.4	34.6	20.3	**31.4**	**51.4**	**39.0**	**30.8**
NER-STYLE																			
zero-shot+*specific*	22.2	1.6	3.0	12.7	5.2	7.4	2.2	1.2	1.6	2.9	0.4	0.7	2.5	2.1	2.3	0.6	0.3	0.4	2.6
5-shot	35.6	31.3	33.3	23.8	54.3	33.1	14.8	32.5	20.4	30.6	27.0	28.7	11.8	36.3	17.8	23.5	31.5	27.0	26.7
+*kNN*	36.0	37.4	36.7	21.6	63.8	32.3	10.3	30.0	15.3	**31.0**	**33.0**	**32.0**	10.4	30.2	15.5	26.3	41.7	32.3	27.4
+*kNN+specific*	**43.7**	**44.7**	**44.2**	**29.9**	**64.8**	**40.9**	11.2	29.2	16.1	30.8	32.8	31.8	9.1	26.6	13.7	29.8	47.3	36.6	30.6
GPT-4*																			
EXTRACT-STYLE	40.7	35.8	38.0	52.4	66.7	58.7	19.7	35.2	25.3	31.1	30.0	30.6	20.8	41.8	27.8	31.9	55.4	40.5	36.8
NER-STYLE	50.9	45.5	48.0	69.0	66.7	67.8	19.4	33.3	24.6	24.2	20.0	21.9	20.4	34.5	25.7	29.0	56.4	38.4	37.7
RELAX	P	R	F1	P	R	F1	P	R	F1	P	R	F1	P	R	F1	P	R	F1	F1
EXTRACT-STYLE																			
5-shot	72.8	67.5	70.0	23.4	70.1	35.0	31.7	**85.7**	**46.3**	**76.1**	65.0	70.1	**34.0**	69.8	45.7	**48.7**	49.1	48.9	52.7
+*kNN*	**82.8**	78.0	80.3	23.2	75.7	35.6	**33.2**	74.3	45.9	74.0	74.0	**74.0**	33.1	76.8	**46.2**	42.2	63.3	50.6	55.4
+*kNN+specific*	80.5	77.2	78.8	34.9	75.9	47.8	33.0	69.5	44.8	72.8	**74.4**	73.6	32.1	**77.4**	45.4	46.5	**76.0**	**57.7**	**58.0**
NER-STYLE																			
5-shot	61.4	53.9	57.4	28.0	63.9	28.9	26.9	59.0	37.0	68.4	60.3	64.1	21.6	66.6	32.6	41.5	55.7	47.6	44.6
+*kNN*	80.5	**83.7**	**82.0**	25.4	74.8	37.9	22.3	65.0	33.2	62.7	66.8	64.7	20.1	58.5	29.9	39.3	62.3	48.2	49.3
+*kNN+specific*	79.4	81.3	80.3	**35.2**	**76.3**	**48.2**	33.0	69.6	44.8	64.0	68.1	66.0	18.6	53.9	27.6	42.0	66.6	51.4	53.1

Table 7: **Results of Experiments.** The metrics are Precision (**P**), Recall (**R**) and span-F1 (**F1**). **For GPT-4, the results are based on a subset of* ≤ 350 *samples for each dataset.*

DATASET		EXTRACT-STYLE	NER-STYLE
FIJO	**Positive**	28.2 / 6 / 2	28.0 / 3 / 8
	Mix	**31.2** / 6 / 4	**29.1** / 5 / 7
KOMPETENCER	**Positive**	**22.9** / 129 / 2	**18.2** / 103 / 4
	Mix	20.1 / 131 / 1	17.8 / 133 / 12
GNEHM	**Positive**	**43.4** / 219 / 11	44.8 / 174 / 11
	Mix	42.2 / 210 / 6	**54.4** / 215 / 17
GREEN	**Positive**	**34.3** / 69 / 21	**35.0** / 17 / 10
	Mix	26.0 / 62 / 17	28.9 / 47 / 17
SKILLSPAN	**Positive**	**31.0** / 212 / 3	17.9 / 125 / 5
	Mix	29.8 / 245 / 7	**20.3** / 183 / 10
SAYFULLINA	**Positive**	**52.2** / 1 / 72	**38.8** / 0 / 36
	Mix	38.5 / 1 / 87	30.3 / 0 / 51
AVG	**Positive**	**35.3**	30.5
	Mix	31.3	30.3

Table 8: Experiments using positive-only demonstrations vs. a mixture of positive-negative. We report **F1 / TN / FN**, with **TN / FN** being the number of true and false negative predictions LLM made (cases where LLM predicted there were no entities).

the **TN** performances for NER-STYLE, while only slightly increasing the number of **FN**. This phenomenon, perhaps, is due to the fact the instruction from EXTRACT-STYLE is obvious and straightforward, from which the LLM can infer the ability to label **None** directly. Therefore, providing LLM with more positive examples solidifies the semantic understanding of the skills extraction task the LLM is solving. Meanwhile, NER-STYLE is very specific in its output and therefore the LLM tends to over-generalize the positive-only NER-format sentences it learns from the in-context demonstrations. Besides, mix demonstrations also results in comparable number of **None** predictions for both EXTRACT-STYLE and NER-STYLE, thus we utilized this approach for our experiments.

B Specific Prompts used for each dataset

The instructions we use for prompting LLMs for each dataset are in Table 9.

C Mismatches types and examples

We provide some examples of common mismatches from skipping/extra spaces and punctuation insertion, as well as examples where the mismatches are based on the pre-trained knowledge of LLMs that can not be modified even with explicit feedback prompt guidance.

Successful sample with minor edits. Minor sentence construction (with regards to punctuations, spaces, and simple grammar errors) that was addressed and fixed by LLMs. Here are a few examples.

Spaces and punctuations:

Original: Test Consultant / Automation Test Analyst will ideally be confident with Selenium and good experience of web based testing , HTML and JavaScript .

DATASET		PROMPT
FIJO	SYSTEM	You are an expert human resource manager in the insurance industry in France. You need to analyse skills required in job offers.
	EXTRACT-STYLE	You are given a sentence from an insurance job description in French. Extract all the skills and competencies that are required from the candidate as list, with one skill per line. If no skill is found in the sentence, return "None".
	NER-STYLE	You are given a sentence from an insurance job description in French. Highlight all the skills and competencies that are required from the candidate, by surrounding them with tags '@@' and '##'. If there are no such element in the sentence, replicate the sentence identically.
KOMPETENCER	SYSTEM	You are an expert human resource manager. You need to analyse skills required in job offers.
	EXTRACT-STYLE	You are given a sentence from a job description in Danish. Extract all the skills, knowledges, and competencies that are required from the candidate as list, with one skill per line. If no skill is found in the sentence, return "None".
	NER-STYLE	You are given a sentence from a job description in Danish. Highlight all the skills, knowledges, and competencies that are required from the candidate, by surrounding them with tags '@@' and '##'. If there are no such element in the sentence, replicate the sentence identically.
GNEHM	SYSTEM	You are an expert human resource manager in information and communication technology (ICT) from Germany. You need to analyse skills required in German job offers.
	EXTRACT-STYLE	You are given a sentence from a job advertisement in German. Extract all the IT/Technology skills and competencies that are required from the candidate as list, with one skill per line. If no skill is found in the sentence, return "None".
	NER-STYLE	You are given an extract from a job advertisement in German. Highlight all the IT/Technology skills and competencies that are required from the candidate, by surrounding them with tags '@@' and '##'. If there are no such element in the sentence, replicate the sentence identically.
GREEN	SYSTEM	You are an expert human resource manager. You need to analyse skills required in job offers.
	EXTRACT-STYLE	You are given a sentence from a job descriptionin various fields like IT, finance, healthcare, and sales. Extract all the skills and competencies that are required from the candidate as list, with one skill per line. If no skill is found in the sentence, return "None"
	NER-STYLE	You are given a sentence from a job description in various fields like IT, finance, healthcare, and sales. Highlight all the skills and competencies that are required from the candidate, by surrounding them with tags '@@' and '##'. If there are no such element in the sentence, replicate the sentence identically.
SKILLSPAN	SYSTEM	You are an expert human resource manager. You need to analyse skills required in job offers.
	EXTRACT-STYLE	You are given a sentence from a job posting. Extract all the skills, knowledges, and competencies that are required from the candidate as list, with one skill per line. If no skill is found in the sentence, return "None".
	NER-STYLE	You are given a sentence from a job posting. Highlight all the skills, knowledges, and competencies that are required from the candidate, by surrounding them with tags '@@' and '##'. If there are no such element in the sentence, replicate the sentence identically.
SAYFULLINA	SYSTEM	You are an expert human resource manager. You need to detect and analyse soft skills required in job offers.
	EXTRACT-STYLE	You are given a sentence from a job advertisement. Extract all the soft skills and competencies that are required from the candidate as list, with one skill per line. If no skill is found in the sentence, return "None"
	NER-STYLE	You are given a sentence from a job advertisement. Highlight all the soft skills and competencies that are required from the candidate, by surrounding them with tags '@@' and '##'. If there are no such element in the sentence, replicate the sentence identically.

Table 9: Full *data-specific* prompts for each dataset.

Generation: @@Test Consultant/Automation Test Analyst## will ideally be confident with @@Selenium## and good experience of @@web based testing##, @@HTML## and @@JavaScript##.

Fixable grammar and vocabulary mistakes:

Original: Sevenoaks , Kent Support Engineer with strong knowledge of Windows and Linux architecture is required by an expanding company based in Sevenoaks to support clients throughout London and Kent .

Generation: @@Support Engineer@@ with @@strong knowledge## of @@Windows## and @@Linux architecture## is required by an expanding company based in Sevenoaks to support clients throughout London and Kent .

Fixed: Sevenoaks , Kent Support Engineer with strong knowledge of @@Windows## and @@Linux architecture## is required by an expanding company based in Sevenoaks to support clients throughout London and Kent .

Failed sample due to common grammar knowledge. LLMs failed to output the exact original sentence because they tend to "over fix" commonly known grammar mistakes. For example, LLMs cannot adhere to the original sentence in the following input, which lacks "To" in "To be considered", even after 3 rounds of feedback loops.

Original: be considered for the General Manager post you will have at least 2years management experience within the health and fitness industry ideally as a General Manager .

Generation: To be considered for the @@General Manager## post you will have at least 2years management experience within the @@health and fitness industry## ideally as a @@General Manager## .

D Qualitative Analysis

We provide examples from datasets GREEN, SKILLSPAN, SAYFULLINA, and FIJO that we believe are more representative of the 60 examples we examined for qualitative analysis in Table 10. We note that this study is highly subjective and does not conform to any specific definition of error categories.

Error Type	Dataset Name	Sentence	Labels	EXTRACT-STYLE	NER-STYLE
Skill definition misalignment	SAYFULLINA	creative and confident when it come to meeting deadlines this could be the	meeting deadlines	creative, confident	creative and confident when it come to meeting deadlines this could be the
Skill definition misalignment	SKILLSPAN	Design and build front-end / BI layer of our data and analytics solutions - Power BI reports DAX queries Azure Analysis Services models .	Design and build front-end / BI layer	Design and build front-end / BI layer of our data and analytics solutions, Power BI reports, DAX queries, Azure Analysis Services models	Design and build front-end / BI layer of our data and analytics solutions - Power BI reports DAX queries Azure Analysis Services models .
Skill definition misalignment	SAYFULLINA	focus , well organize with excellent communication and organizational skills	organizational skills	focus, organizational skills	focus , well organize with excellent @@communication## and @@organizational## skills
Conjoined skill	SKILLSPAN	Optimize and manage existing reward and benefits programmes and processes to support the business priorities and ensure local compliance.	Optimize and manage existing reward and benefits programmes and processes, support the business priorities, ensure local compliance	optimize reward and benefits programmes, manage reward and benefits processes, support business priorities, ensure local compliance	@@Optimize and manage existing reward and benefits programmes and processes## to @@support the business priorities## and @@ensure local compliance## .
Conjoined skill	GREEN	leading manufacturing business who supply luxury products to the Retail and Leisure industries are looking to recruit a talented Supply Chain Manager to manage operations , production , warehousing , delivery , reporting and to develop best practice Supply Chain procedures within the organisation .	delivery, develop best practice Supply Chain procedures, warehousing, manage operations, reporting, production	Supply Chain Manager, operations, production, warehousing, delivery, reporting, develop best practice Supply Chain procedures	leading manufacturing business who supply luxury products to the Retail and Leisure industries are looking to recruit a talented Supply Chain Manager to @@manage operations## , @@production## , @@warehousing## , @@delivery## , @@reporting## and to @@develop best practice Supply Chain procedures## within the organisation .
Extended Span	GREEN	Frank International is the leading Microsoft Dynamics recruitment firm in the UK , advertising more Dynamics CRM jobs than any other agency .	Microsoft Dynamics, Dynamics CRM	Microsoft Dynamics recruitment, Dynamics CRM jobs	Frank International is the leading @@Microsoft Dynamics recruitment firm## in the UK , advertising more @@Dynamics CRM jobs## than any other agency .
Extended Span	GREEN	to degree level ideally in business strong relationship builder organise and analytical polish	relationship builder	strong relationship builder, organise, analytical	to degree level ideally in business @@strong relationship builder## organise and analytical polish
Wrong annotations	GREEN	will still be part of an office team with all the community and collective achievement that goes with that . This	be part of an office team	None	will still be part of an office team with all the @@community## and @@collective achievement## that goes with that . This
Wrong annotations	SAYFULLINA	any offer be subject to rigorous reference , criminal and credit check	rigorous	rigorous reference, credit check	any offer be subject to rigorous @@reference## , @@criminal## and @@credit check##
Wrong extraction	SKILLSPAN	You will be a part of a small team of 4 people in the division who closely cooperate with our <LOCATION> <LOCATION> office in the development process .		cooperate with our <LOCATION> <LOCATION> office	You will be a part of a small team of 4 people in the division who closely cooperate with our @@<LOCATION> <LOCATION> office## in the development process .
Wrong extraction	SAYFULLINA	be willing to travel solo internationally infrequently have	willing to travel	None	be willing to travel solo internationally infrequently @@have##

Table 10: Qualitative examples failed extractions for each category. LLM sometimes cannot conform to the strict NER-output requirements, even though its extraction makes sense.

Prompt	Dataset	Span Length Difference	Number of Skills Difference
NER	GREEN	2.15	-0.03
	SKILLSPAN	2.32	-0.49
	FIJO	-2.25	-0.06
	SAYFULLINA	3.54	-0.56
	KOMPETENCER	3.12	-0.49
	GNEHM	3.72	-0.36
NER	avg	2.10	-0.33
EXTRACT	green	1.28	-0.04
	SKILLSPAN	1.31	-0.43
	FIJO	-2.81	0.10
	SAYFULLINA	3.32	-0.64
	KOMPETENCER	2.03	-0.44
	GNEHM	3.64	-0.41
EXTRACT	avg	1.46	-0.31

Table 11: Difference between skills extracted by GPT-3.5 and gold annotations, for each dataset and prompting strategy. We use kNN-5-shots with dataset-specific prompts.

JobSkape: A Framework for Generating Synthetic Job Postings to Enhance Skill Matching

Antoine Magron[*1] Anna Dai[*1] Mike Zhang[2]
Syrielle Montariol[1] Antoine Bosselut[1]
[1]EPFL, Switzerland
[2]IT University of Copenhagen, Denmark
syrielle.montariol@epfl.ch mikejj.zhang@gmail.com

Abstract

Recent approaches in skill matching, employing synthetic training data for classification or similarity model training, have shown promising results, reducing the need for time-consuming and expensive annotations. However, previous synthetic datasets have limitations, such as featuring only one skill per sentence and generally comprising short sentences. In this paper, we introduce JobSkape, a framework to generate synthetic data that tackles these limitations, specifically designed to enhance skill-to-taxonomy matching. Within this framework, we create SkillSkape, a comprehensive open-source synthetic dataset of job postings tailored for skill-matching tasks. We introduce several offline metrics that show that our dataset resembles real-world data. Additionally, we present a multi-step pipeline for skill extraction and matching tasks using large language models (LLMs), benchmarking against known supervised methodologies. We outline that the downstream evaluation results on real-world data can beat baselines, underscoring its efficacy and adaptability. [1]

1 Introduction

In the dynamic modern labor market, understanding job demands at scale is crucial for informed decision-making by policymakers, businesses, and other stakeholders. One way of measuring job market demand lies in *skill matching*: the extraction and alignment of skills from job descriptions to their disambiguated forms (i.e., a knowledge base or taxonomy). This process facilitates the investigation of current labor market dynamics and the quantification of labor market demands, addressing the occupational skill matching problem.

Regardless of their predictive effectiveness, supervised learning methods for skill matching require regularly collecting and annotating up-to-date data (Zhang et al., 2022b), a process that is both expensive and time-consuming. Synthetic data circumvents the need for such costly annotations. However, despite efforts in generating synthetic training data (Clavié and Soulié, 2023; Decorte et al., 2023) and real-world benchmarks (Zhang et al., 2022a; Decorte et al., 2022), challenges like incoherent sentences and over-simplified setups exist in existing datasets. To address these shortcomings, we introduce JobSkape, a framework for generating realistic skill matching datasets that can be used for training and benchmarking.

JobSkape facilitates the creation of diverse labeled textual datasets that align closely with actual job postings, ensuring cleaner and more coherent data. We demonstrate its practical application by generating SkillSkape, a large-scale dataset linking coherent sets of skills to corresponding job descriptions. JobSkape uses generative large language models (LLMs) to curate meaningful skill combinations and generate appropriate job descriptions containing these combinations. A self-refinement step using LLMs (Madaan et al., 2023) ensures label quality in the refined SkillSkape dataset, assessed through offline metrics. Finally, we challenge traditional supervised skill matching methods with an LLM-based, in-context learning (ICL) pipeline, to circumvent re-training the supervised model given new data. We evaluate skill matching performance on our synthetic dataset and real-world annotated data (Decorte et al., 2022), comparing our proposed extraction and matching pipeline with supervised matching models trained on our dataset as well as previous generation attempts (Decorte et al., 2023) in a controlled setting.

Contributions. In this work, we contribute the following: (1) we propose JobSkape, a framework for generating a synthetic dataset of job de-

[*]Equal contribution.

[1]Code and data available at `https://github.com/magantoine/JobSkape`

Proceedings of the First Workshop on Natural Language Processing for Human Resources (NLP4HR 2024), pages 43–58
March 22, 2024 ©2024 Association for Computational Linguistics

scriptions for skill matching with existing skill taxonomies, (2) using our framework, we release a synthetic train and evaluation dataset (SKILLSKAPE) for skill matching, (3) we show that SKILLSKAPE has higher textual quality measured in perplexity and implicitness compared to previous synthetic datasets, (4) lastly, we introduce an ICL-based approach to extract and match skills from job descriptions to a taxonomy and show that this method can outperform supervised baselines on real-world benchmarks.

2 Related Work

Synthetic Data Generation. Traditional synthetic data generation relies on language models, where a generator model is trained on an existing dataset and then employed to generate new data (Mohapatra and Mohapatra, 2022; Kumar et al., 2020). More recent unsupervised methods, such as Wang et al. (2021), leverage pre-trained language models like GPT-3 (Brown et al., 2020) without the need for explicit supervision. Other examples include Ye et al. (2022); Gao et al. (2023), who use carefully designed prompts for data generation. Honovich et al. (2022) generate synthetic instructions for fine-tuning large language models, while Shao et al. (2023) create synthetic demonstrations to enhance the performance of prompting LLMs.

Synthetic Data for Job Postings. In the job market domain, Decorte et al. (2023); Clavié and Soulié (2023) both employ GPT-3.5/4 to generate synthetic training data for skill matching. Specifically, Decorte et al. (2023) prompt GPT-4 to generate ten examples for each ESCO skill, while Clavié and Soulié (2023) use GPT-3.5 to generate 40 examples for each ESCO skill. In this work, we compare our dataset with the one from Decorte et al. (2023), referred to hereafter as the DECORTE dataset.

Skill Matching. Earlier works focus on standardizing skills through matching with taxonomies. For supervised methods, Gnehm et al. (2022) extract skills from Swiss-German job descriptions and match them with the ESCO taxonomy in a two-step process. Zhang et al. (2022b) assume pre-extracted skills and classify spans into their respective taxonomy codes using multiclass classification. Decorte et al. (2022) use distant supervision with the ESCO taxonomy to obtain labels, employ binary classifiers for each ESCO skill and enhance training through negative sampling strategies. Decorte et al. (2023); Clavié and Soulié (2023) employ LLMs for skill matching with ESCO. Decorte et al. (2023) generate a synthetic training set using GPT-3.5 and optimize a bi-encoder through contrastive training for matching. Clavié and Soulié (2023) use a similar approach, generating synthetic training data and employing a linear classifier for each skill with a negative sampling strategy. Additionally, they use sentence embedders (Reimers and Gurevych, 2019) to measure the similarity between extracted skills and ESCO.

3 The JOBSKAPE Framework

Our goal is to create a synthetic dataset comprising job posting sentences associated with lists of skills from a taxonomy that closely aligns with real-world job posting sentences. We initiate the process by generating combinations of skills, derived from a given taxonomy, that are likely to coexist in a job description. Leveraging LLMs and refinement techniques, we produce diverse, realistic, and accurate job description sentences. To evaluate the quality of our synthetic data generation, we define a set of offline metrics and compare the generated sentences with real job postings.

3.1 The Label Space

In this study, we use the European Skills, Competences, Qualifications, and Occupations (ESCO; le Vrang et al., 2014) taxonomy as the label space. ESCO comprises 13,890 competencies categorized into *Skill*, *Knowledge*, and *Attitudes*. Knowledge, according to ESCO, involves assimilating information through learning, encompassing facts, principles, theories, and practices in a specific field of work or study.[2] For example, acquiring proficiency in the Python programming language through learning represents a *knowledge* component, classified as a *hard skill*. Conversely, the application of this knowledge to perform tasks is considered a *skill* component, defined by ESCO as the ability to apply knowledge and use know-how to accomplish tasks and solve problems.[3] For the synthetic sentence generation task at hand, we do not distinguish between skill and knowledge components.

Our synthetic dataset creation framework generates sentences containing multiple skills listed in

[2] https://ec.europa.eu/esco/portal/escopedia/Knowledge

[3] https://ec.europa.eu/esco/portal/escopedia/Skill

the ESCO taxonomy. To reduce the data generation cost (and to facilitate a fair comparison with prior work), we use the same subset of 514 ESCO skills used in SKILLSPAN-M, an annotated set of real-world job postings.

3.2 Formal Approach

Previous efforts (Decorte et al., 2023; Clavié and Soulié, 2023) focused on generating synthetic training sentences with a single skill. In contrast, we advocate for sentences containing multiple relevant skills to resemble sentences from real job postings. We initiate the process by creating combinations of skills, guided by three main conditions:

1. **Varying Lengths of Skill Combination**: Recognizing the heterogeneity in real-world job postings, we incorporate varying numbers of skills per sentence. By doing so, our sentences will show higher diversity similar to real job advertisements.

2. **Semantic Closeness in Skill Pairing**: In real job postings, skills that are mentioned in the same sentence are often related to each other. Aligning with the logical grouping of skills, we construct more realistic and contextually coherent sentences.

3. **Minimum Skill Representation**: While our dataset aims to reflect the real-world frequency of skill occurrences, we also want to ensure that each skill appears enough times for training. This guarantees that even less common skills are adequately represented, creating a more effective training dataset.

To achieve variety, we introduce two distributions, $\mathcal{N}$ (distribution of combination size) and $\mathcal{F}$ (distribution describing skill frequency in job postings, akin to skill popularity). We iteratively process skills $s_i \in \mathcal{S}$, the set of skills in our taxonomy, ensuring each skill has the same minimum number of samples. For each skill, we identify its k nearest neighbors $\{s'_j\}_{j=1}^{k}$ based on cosine similarity between embeddings obtained from JobBERT, a language model fine-tuned on domain-specific data (Zhang et al., 2022a). Neighbors with a similarity above threshold T are retained, forming the set of nearest neighbors $\mathcal{S}_i$:

$$\mathcal{S}_i = \{s_j : s_j \in \{s'_i\}_{i=1}^{k} \wedge \text{sim}(s_j, s_i)\}T\}. \quad (1)$$

This set is used for skill combination selection. We draw a sample size n from distribution $\mathcal{N}$, setting the combination size to $min(n, |\mathcal{S}_i|)$. However, sampling skills directly from $\mathcal{S}_i$ is not straightforward. For instance, in analyzing the top nearest neighbors of *SQL*, a frequently occurring skill in job postings, we find *THC Hydra*, which is much less common. To accurately replicate the real-world frequency distribution of skills in our synthetic dataset, we adjust sampling probabilities to reflect actual skill popularity. Hence, we introduce distribution $\mathcal{F}$ to compute the probability of selection over $\mathcal{S}_i$ using softmax:

$$\mathbf{P}(s_j) = \frac{e^{\mathbf{P}_{\mathcal{F}}(s_j)}}{\sum_{l=1}^{k} e^{\mathbf{P}_{\mathcal{F}}(s_l)}}. \quad (2)$$

where $\mathbf{P}_{\mathcal{F}}(s_i)$ is the popularity of the skill s_i. We then select $min(n, |\mathcal{S}_i|)$ skills from $\mathcal{S}_i$ using the computed probability distribution.

For dataset creation, we form skill combinations from our ESCO subset, with $\mathcal{N}$ set to $U(1, 5)$. We employ JobBERT to obtain domain-specific embeddings for job descriptions and skills. The distribution $\mathcal{F}$ is computed as the average of standardized negative perplexities across sentences generated with GPT-2 (Radford et al., 2019). These sentences include variations like "`I want a job that involves {skill}`", "`For my job, I want to learn [to] {skills}`", "`At my job, my main is skill is [to] {skill}`", ensuring grammatical correctness. We set a similarity threshold T to 0.83 to be closer to SkillSpan distribution, using $k = 20$.

3.3 Prompt Tuning for Generation

Given a skill combination, we generate synthetic job description sentences. A candidate for this hypothetical job would need to be proficient to some extent in each of these skills. We use GPT-3.5 as the text generator. We describe two types of generations:

- **Dense**: For a combination of four or less skills we generate a short job description of at most one sentence. This is done to minimize the number of hallucinated skills that could appear when generating a long job description with a small set of skills.
- **Sparse**: For a combination of more than four skills, we generate a job description paragraph containing multiple sentences. The information is more "sparse".

Our prompt follows Clavié and Soulié (2023), it is used to make the mentions of the skills as implicit as possible (i.e., skill does not have an exact string match in the text). We further enhance the diversity by prompting the model to vary the openings of the descriptions and avoid the examples starting with "`We are looking`" or "`We are searching`" (see Appendix A.3.1).

We add additional instructions to the prompt to reduce ambiguity. To each prompt, we add a list of synonyms of each inputted skill that are in the taxonomy and instruct the model to not refer to *SQL* as *MySQL* since *MySQL* is a separate skill in the taxonomy. Each skill is also given along with their respective definitions to give more context to the model and avoid miscomprehension.

3.4 Refinement of SKILLSKAPE

At this step, the dataset comprises exclusively of positive samples, which means that every generated sentence contains at least one associated skill. To train a supervised classifier for real job descriptions, negative samples – sentences containing unknown skills or no skills – are required. To create negative samples with unknown skills, we apply the same generation method as positive samples but draw from a broader pool of skills. This pool includes skills that are not in our selected list but known in the wider skill universe. We also generate negative samples containing no skills to represent sentences in real-life job ads that do not mention skills required from the candidate. To do so, we use two separate prompts to generate (1) sentences describing the company: its reach, domain, location, et cetera and (2) sentences detailing the salary and perks of a job (see Appendix A.3.2). To guide the model in the generation, we provide two demonstrations. For the SKILLSKAPE dataset, we generate 500 negative samples with unknown skills as well as 500 additional negative samples containing no skills.

We then apply self-refinement (Madaan et al., 2023), involving feeding the generated sentences back into the same model for feedback. The model is asked to extract skills using the pipeline described in Appendix A.4.1, matching them with the taxonomy. We compare the generated set of skills with the gold set of skills, adding to the gold list all skills that were found in the sentence. We do this because the LLM can extrapolate during sentence generation, thereby adding related skills on top of the original list that was fed to it. The list of skills, along with their associated spans in the sentences, is filtered to include only pairs of skills and spans that have a cosine similarity above a specified threshold. For this refined dataset version, we use JobBERT as a span encoder, and the threshold is empirically set to 0.7 cosine similarity. One of the main reasons for this low similarity is the LLM not reflecting accurately the gold skill during the sentence generation step. In that case, we wish to remove that skill from the gold set of skills associated with the sentence.

Span Extraction. We use GPT-3.5 to label skill sequences in the sentences. Each mention, whether implicit or explicit, is surrounded by `@@` and `##` following Wang et al. (2023). In case the language model fails to label the span, it is asked to self-correct, as outlined in Appendix A.4.2. We showcase two examples extracted from the training set of the refined SKILLSKAPE dataset.

Positive example. This 28-word example, average in length for our dataset, contains three key skills as annotated spans required of the applicant.

> **Sentence**: The ideal candidate will effectively @@engage with upper-level management##, @@maintain strong communication channels with key stakeholders##, and @@collaborate with peers## to ensure seamless coordination throughout the organization.
>
> **Label**: 'liaise with managers', 'communicate with stakeholders', 'liaise with colleagues'

In the example, the inter-skill similarity is high, showcasing the efficiency of the skill combination selection method.

Negative example. This sentence mentions information about the hiring company instead of the job itself, and therefore, contains no skills.

> **Sentence**: Embrace a challenging and fulfilling career with us, where your hard work is recognized through a salary range of $80,000 to $90,000, reflecting our appreciation for your contributions.
>
> **Label**: NO LABEL

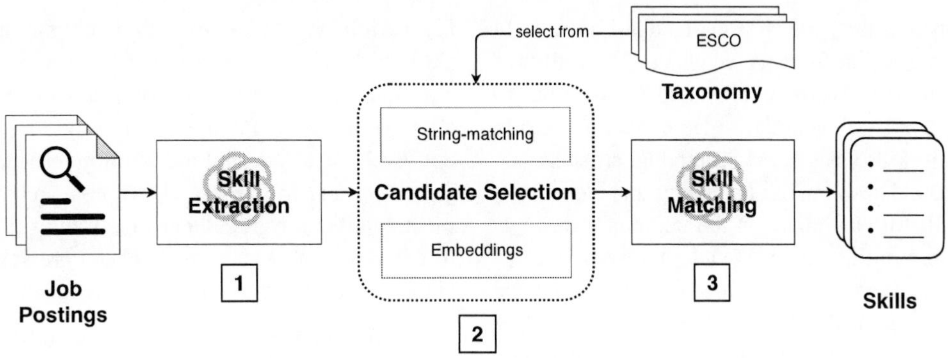

Figure 1: **Three-step Skill Extraction and Matching Pipeline**. We show our in-context learning pipeline for end-to-end skill matching. We use an LLM to extract skills from job ads, then do candidate selection using heuristics, and last, do skill matching with a constrained taxonomy.

Dataset	Split	Avg. # Skills	% UNKs	Avg. # Words	# Samples
SKILLSPAN-M	Dev.	2.0	47.0	15.0	178
	Test	1.9	47.3	16.3	751
DECORTE	Train	1.0	0.2	15.7	5,120
SKILLSKAPE	Train	2.6	7.9	28.2	6,352
	Dev.	2.1	8.3	27.8	1,316
	Test	2.6	8.4	28.1	1,272

Table 1: **Datasets' Statistics.** Average # skills and words refer to the average per sample (job posting sentence(s) and % UNKs refer to the percentage of skill labels are under the unknown UNK label.

3.5 Summary and Comparison

The final version of SKILLSKAPE has 8940 samples, split into training, development and test sets (~ 70-15-15 split). We provide several descriptive statistics in Table 1. To assess the quality of our generations, we compare the generated dataset SKILLSKAPE with two other datasets from the literature: (1) a manually annotated benchmark, created by Decorte et al. (2022), based on the SKILLSPAN-M(ATCH) dataset (Zhang et al., 2022a), which contains over 14.5K job posting sentences scraped from various sources, and (2) the DECORTE dataset (Decorte et al., 2023), synthetically generated from ESCO using GPT-4. By design, we created SKILLSKAPE to cover the same label space as SKILLSPAN-M, which has only a development and a test set. In that dataset, two labels are used to indicate skills without an adapted label in the taxonomy: UNDERSPECIFIED and LABEL NOT PRESENT. We map these to the UNK label used in SKILLSKAPE. DECORTE associates ten synthetic sentences to each skill in the ESCO taxonomy. It is only used as training data. It covers all of ESCO (13.9K skills), but we restrict it to sentences with skills occurring in SKILLSPAN-M, leading to 5,120 samples (we add 10 random UNK sentences).

4 Experimental Setup

In this section, we introduce several benchmarks for skill matching tasks. We train a supervised multi-label classifier and present an LLM-based approach with in-context learning.

4.1 Supervised Multi-label Classifier

For the supervised baseline, we use a pre-trained $\text{BERT}_{base\_uncased}$ model (Devlin et al., 2019) to extract contextualized embeddings from the input text $t = \{w_1, w_2, ..., w_n\}$. These embeddings are then input into a multi-label classifier with a sigmoid activation applied independently to each output logit. Let $y = \{y_1, y_2, ..., y_k\}$ represent binary labels for the k classes. The model predicts the labels using:

$$\hat{y}_i = \sigma(f_i(\text{BERT}(\boldsymbol{t}))), \quad (3)$$

where $f_i(\cdot)$ is a function that maps the output embeddings from BERT to a logit for class i, $\sigma(\cdot)$ is the sigmoid activation, and $\hat{y}_i$ is the predicted probability for class i. The probability threshold can be tuned; we empirically found that 0.2 works well for this task.

We train the BERT_{base} model for 100 epochs with a learning rate of 3×10^{-5} and select the best-performing epoch. We use a batch size of 16 and a maximum sequence length of 128. The model is trained for five different seeds.

4.2 In-context Learning with LLMs

We leverage an LLM to match skills in synthetic job posting sentences to the ESCO taxonomy. This pipeline has three steps, visualized in Figure 1: 1) **skill extraction** from the sentence, 2) **candidate selection** from the taxonomy, and 3) **skill matching** to the list of candidates. Here, we first extract relevant skills using LLM-prompting, pre-select viable candidates from our taxonomy, and then match the skills to candidates in the taxonomy through LLM-prompting again. We adopt a three-step approach to overcome the limited context window of LLMs, specifically 4K for `GPT-3.5-turbo` (OpenAI, 2023), which makes feeding large taxonomies directly to the model impractical.

(1) Skill Extraction. For each job posting, the LLM identifies key skills and tasks within the job ad while omitting irrelevant information. The LLM is directed to respond by repeating the sentence and tagging the skills by surrounding them with `@@` and ##, following Wang et al. (2023), as shown in our prompt below.

```
System: You are an expert human resource manager. You need to analyse skills in a job posting.

Instruction: You are an expert human resource manager. You are given an extract from a job description. Highlight all the skills, competencies and tasks that are required from the candidate applying for the job, by surrounding them with tags @@ and ##. Make sure you don't highlight job titles, nor elements related to the company and not to the job itself. Make sure to rewrite the sentence with all the tags.

{Demontrations}

Sentence: {Sentence}

Answer:
```

We provide seven demonstrations in a few-shot setting to assist the model in understanding the task and following the instructions. To select few-shot examples, we use kNN retrieval from a training set composed of sentences along with their spans and labels (Liu et al., 2022). The closest samples from our dataset are selected as few-shot examples (see Appendix A). Finally, We process the output by extracting the tagged sections as skills.

(2) Candidate Selection. Matching extracted skills with skills defined in the taxonomy is crucial. Each skill in the taxonomy is associated with a tiered structure of names, each providing different levels of detail, and a definition. To provide richer context to the model, we concatenate the most detailed (or granular) name of the skill with its definition. We use two methods for pre-selecting viable candidates from the taxonomy for each skill:

- **`rule-based`**: Through string matching, we seek full or approximate matches of the extracted skill within the taxonomy. If the exact string of the extracted skill is present in the name or definition of a skill in the taxonomy, it is considered a good candidate for a match. We randomly select five entries if more than five candidates are found. If the exact strings do not match, we calculate the `token_set_ratio` using TheFuzz,[4] a similarity score based on Levenshtein's distance (Levenshtein et al., 1966). The top five candidates with the highest scores are chosen.
- **`embedding-based`**: Using a pre-trained language model (JobBERT; Zhang et al., 2022a), we compare the extracted skills with taxonomy entries. We obtain the contextualized embeddings of the extracted skill by embedding the sentences and averaging the vector representation of the tokens of the extracted skill. These embeddings are then compared to the representation of each skill in the ESCO taxonomy if the extracted skill is a substring of the sentences it was extracted from. Otherwise, the embedding of the extracted skill itself is compared to the skills in the taxonomy. The top five most similar candidates are selected based on cosine similarity.

While effective, the rule-based method may miss synonyms and context. On the other hand, the embedding-based method addresses the limitations of the rule-based method but risks selecting contextually similar yet factually dissimilar candidates (e.g., software vs. hardware). Therefore, we adopt a hybrid approach, retaining candidates from both rule-based and embedding-based methods.

(3) Skill Matching. The final step involves matching extracted skills to one of the selected candidate skills. We present the LLM with formatted candidates as options, and request the best

[4] `https://github.com/seatgeek/thefuzz`

	Perplexity (↓)	S2SIM (↑)	Explicitness (%, ↓)
SKILLSPAN-M	178.2	0.662	5.0
DECORTE	65.1	0.739	22.4
SKILLSKAPE	44.3	0.744	6.9

Table 2: **Offline Metrics.** We show the offline metrics as described in Subsection 4.3. (↑) indicates higher the better, (↓) indicates lower is better.

match, resembling a ranking task. The model outputs the most fitting option as a matched skill or provides no match if none are found. To assist the model without overloading the prompt, we provide a one-shot example in the following format:

```
Sentence: {generated sentence}
Skill: {extracted span}
A: {candidate 1}
...
J: {candidate 10}
Answer: {selected candidate}
```

The full prompt with one-shot demontration can be found in Appendix A.2.

To conduct the experiments for in-context learning with LLM, we retrieve demonstrations from the training set to provide examples for both the extraction and matching steps. We conduct an ablation study on SkillSpan's validation set to select the best number of shots for both tasks. Experiments are described in Appendix B, in Table 4, and Figure 2. The matching step is performed with 10 candidates using the mixed setting (5 embedding candidates and 5 string matching candidates). The best setting uses 7 demonstrations for the extraction step and one demonstration for the matching step. Matching step demonstrations have a large number of tokens due to the list of candidates along with their definitions, which can explain the decreased performance associated with adding more demonstrations.

4.3 Offline Quality Metrics

We design a set of metrics to evaluate the quality and diversity of the data at hand. Our intention is not to mirror metrics of SKILLSPAN-M, which is untidy by nature of scraped data, but to produce high-quality training data for downstream skill matching tasks.

1. First, we consider **Perplexity**, i.e., how realistic the data is from the point of view of a language model. We compute the perplexity of each of the sentences using GPT-2 (Radford et al., 2019), where lower is better.
2. Second, we consider **Skill-Sentence Similarity (S2SIM)**, the average cosine similarity between a skill and the associated sentence. The higher this metric, the closer the generated sentence will be semantically close to the associated skills. We aim to maximize this metric. The embeddings are computed using JobBERT, and BERT model fine-tuned on English job postings with the masked language modeling objective.
3. Finally, we measure **Explicitness** by counting the number of entities that appear exactly in the sample, using string matching.

Table 2 shows offline metrics for SKILLSPAN-M, DECORTE, and SKILLSKAPE. SKILLSKAPE has a lower perplexity, and outperforms SKILLSPAN and DECORTE in terms of S2SIM. The main reason for SKILLSPAN-M's low skill-sentence similarity is its noisiness, leading to sentences often being cut mid-way and lacking coherence. Around 7% of SKILLSKAPE skills are fully explicit (the label can be found exactly in the sentence), much closer to SKILLSPAN-M than DECORTE. A higher explicitness leads to an easier task; a skill matching model needs to be trained on enough implicit examples to allow it to generalize to implicit skills.

Overall, SKILLSKAPE demonstrates similar statistics in perplexity and S2SIM characteristics as DECORTE. However, it notably exhibits a significant (3×) enhancement in implicitly representing skills within each sentence.

5 Results and Analysis

To assess the label refinement method (Section 3.4), we apply it to the development set of the SKILLSPAN-M benchmark that has annotated skills and associated spans. 40% of our extracted spans match exactly with the annotated span. 60% of our extracted spans are either a perfect match or contain the annotated span. In general, extracted spans have a Jaccard similarity of 62% with the annotated spans.

5.1 Supervised vs. Few-shot ICL Matching

In Table 3, we show the results of the skill matching task on the SKILLSPAN-M test set and SKILLSKAPE test set. We compare the performance of supervised and in-context learning methods *trained*

↓Train / Test→	Supervised		Few-Shot ICL	
	SKILLSKAPE	SKILLSPAN-M	SKILLSKAPE	SKILLSPAN-M
DECORTE	28.0 ± 0.8	23.0 ± 0.7	36.8 ± 0.2	26.9 ± 0.5
SKILLSKAPE	**68.0 ± 0.5**	22.2 ± 0.9	**37.6 ± 0.2**	26.9 ± 0.3
Both	67.2 ± 1.0	**26.1 ± 1.2**	**37.6 ± 0.2**	**27.3 ± 0.4**

Table 3: **Supervised and Few-Shot ICL Results.** *Both* indicates the concatenation of DECORTE and SKILLSKAPE. The scores are micro-F_1.

on the DECORTE training set, SKILLSKAPE training set, or the concatenation of both. The supervised approach uses training data to train a supervised multi-label classifier, whereas the few-shot ICL approach uses it as a demonstration pool to retrieve kNN demonstrations. For simplicity, we refer to both training and few-shot learning with demonstrations as *training* in the remainder of this section.

Comparing across supervised and few-shot in-context learning settings, we observe that both supervised and ICL approaches achieve higher performance on both real-world data (SKILLSPAN-M) and our synthetic dataset (SKILLSKAPE) when trained on SKILLSKAPE training set or a combination of SKILLSKAPE and DECORTE training sets. This increase in matching performance is likely due to a higher textual diversity in the SKILLSKAPE dataset. Across both matching approaches, we also observe that training on both SKILLSKAPE and DECORTE consistently achieves the highest test F_1 scores on real-world data. However, the difference in performance is greater for the supervised approach than ICL, highlighting that the ability to generate high-quality data is most impactful for supervised approaches.

Additionally, we observe an interesting result in the large difference between the supervised and ICL performance on the SKILLSKAPE test set, 68.0/67.2 and 37.6 micro-F_1 respectively when trained on SKILLSKAPE or a combination of SKILLSKAPE and DECORTE. We suspect that this difference could largely be due the characteristics of our training and test data. Supervised models tend to perform well when the training and test data follow the same distributions. In contrast, the few-shot ICL method consistently outperforms than the supervised approach on the SKILLSPAN-M test set. Given the minimal tuning required for the ICL method, the ICL approach can be better suited to flexibly handle messy real-world data. These results suggest that, for use cases when we have a sample of annotated data from the same distribution as the data we want to predict, we can combine it with synthetic training data and leverage supervised models. Otherwise, the in-context learning approach is less dependent on the training data.

In Appendix Table 6, we show several qualitative examples of predictions of both the multi-label classifier and LLM. Several noticeable patterns are underprediction for the multi-label classifier and overprediction of the LLM. Additionally, we notice that the predictions of both models are rather close "semantically" to the gold labels, but are deemed incorrect by the evaluation.

In summary, the results underscore the significance of both the quantity and diversity of training data in the development of effective skill matching dataset generators.

5.2 Effect of In-context Demonstrations

We evaluate the sensitivity of our method to the number and candidate selection methodology of in-context learning examples.

Demonstrations. We perform an ablation study on the number of demonstrations for both skill extraction and matching. Results in Appendix Table 4 show that 7 shots for extraction with 1 shot for matching leads to the best performance.

Candidate Selection. Candidate selection using the hybrid method for $n = 5$ candidates from each of the rules- and embedding-based methods (i.e., 10 candidates in Figure 3) presents the best trade-off between performance and computational cost. While we do observe a higher F_1 score as we increase the number of candidates, the increase in performance appears to be marginal while it would more than double the number of input tokens.

Finally, an ablation study on the matching step of the pipeline (see AppendixB.3) shows that directly selecting the top-1 candidate (rule-based) as skill prediction lags behind the performance of using GPT-3.5 as a re-ranker by around 8% F_1.

5.3 Effect of Sentence Length

The sentence length distribution is heavily skewed toward shorter sentences in the DECORTE and SKILLSPAN-M test sets, with 50% of sentences being 13–19 words in DECORTE and 7–20 words in SKILLSPAN-M. In contrast, 50% of the sentences in SKILLSKAPE are between 23–33 words (see Figure 4 in Appendix for a visualization of the length distribution for each dataset).

When splitting the SKILLSPAN-M test set into two equal-sized sets depending on the size of the sequence (less than 12 words, or more than 12 words), training on DECORTE leads to slightly higher performance than SKILLSKAPE for shorter sentences (0.26 vs. 0.24 F_1). For longer sentences, however, SKILLSKAPE reaches an F_1-score of 0.18 while Decorte's F_1 is 0.17.

6 Conclusion

We introduce JOBSKAPE, a general framework for generating synthetic job posting sentences for skill matching. Using our framework, we release SKILLSKAPE a large dataset of synthetic job posting sentences labeled with ESCO skills. Our analysis shows that SKILLSKAPE contains more implicit skills, has longer sentences, and is overall closer to real-world data, compared to alternative synthetic dataset from the literature. Using our dataset, we conducted several skill matching experiments by training a supervised multi-label classifier and using in-context learning with an LLM, and showed that both methods achieved comparable results when evaluated on real-world data (F_1 of 26.1 and 27.3 respectively). Furthermore, we note that the potential applications of JOBSKAPE extend beyond its current scope. Its application in creating synthetic CVs, for instance, can enhance job matching algorithms and facilitate skill-gap analysis in various industries. The framework's adaptability to different skill taxonomies also opens up possibilities for use across multiple sectors. While promising, these extended applications require further exploration to fully assess their impact.

7 Limitations

Closed model. One of the primary limitations comes from our use of Large Language Models (LLMs) that are closed. This restricts our ability to understand, modify, or customize the underlying mechanisms of these models. The closed nature of the LLMs used in our study also limits the transparency, adaptability, and reproducibility of our system.

English only. Our method is limited to processing and understanding English language content. This language-specific focus narrows the scope of our system's applicability, excluding non-English speaking demographics.

Bias inherited from LLMs. Another significant limitation is the potential bias inherited from the LLMs. Since these models are trained on large datasets that may contain biases, there is a risk that our system may inadvertently perpetuate these biases in its generations. This could manifest in various forms, such as gender, cultural, or industry-specific biases, and could affect the fairness and neutrality of the job postings generated. Furthermore, if biased postings are used extensively, they could adversely influence downstream tasks. For example, biased job postings could skew job recommendation algorithms, leading to unfair job suggestions that do not treat all individuals equally. This highlights the need for careful consideration and mitigation of biases in our approach to ensure equitable outcomes in all applications.

Subset of the Taxonomy. Due to limited resources, we restricted the generation of our synthetic dataset to $\sim$8K samples, with a fraction of the ESCO taxonomy that is also used in the SKILLSPAN-M dataset. Consequently, the multi-class classifier is also trained to classify with a limited set of skills. Scaling up to the full taxonomy might modify the behavior of the supervised classification model, while it should have little to no impact on the ICL skill-matching pipeline.

8 Ethics Statement

In this work, we strictly used publicly available data and generated synthetic datasets, avoiding the use of sensitive or private information. This approach aligns with ethical standards concerning data privacy and security.

However, our system can be used to extract information from personal documents, or be used for sensitive applications in the human resources domain, notably pre-selecting candidates to hire. It shall not be used without the supervision of a human. In this work, we focus on the development of a framework to reduce reliance on real-world annotated data. Extended to resumes, it could allow users to perform the skill extraction and matching task without requiring personal data to be anonymized. Given the limited performance of anonymization tools, generating data following similar distribution would greatly reduce privacy issues for such applications.

Acknowledgements

We thank Jibril Frej (EPFL) for fruitful discussions and feedback on the first version of the paper. MZ is supported by the Independent Research Fund Denmark (DFF) grant 9131-00019B and in parts by ERC Consolidator Grant DIALECT 101043235. We also gratefully acknowledge the support of the Swiss National Science Foundation (No. 215390), Innosuisse (PFFS-21-29), the EPFL Science Seed Fund, the EPFL Center for Imaging, Sony Group Corporation, and the Allen Institute for AI.

References

Tom Brown, Benjamin Mann, Nick Ryder, Melanie Subbiah, Jared D Kaplan, Prafulla Dhariwal, Arvind Neelakantan, Pranav Shyam, Girish Sastry, Amanda Askell, et al. 2020. Language models are few-shot learners. *Advances in neural information processing systems*, 33:1877–1901.

Benjamin Clavié and Guillaume Soulié. 2023. Large language models as batteries-included zero-shot ESCO skills matchers. In *Proceedings of the 3rd Workshop on Recommender Systems for Human Resources (RecSys in HR 2023) co-located with the 17th ACM Conference on Recommender Systems (RecSys 2023), Singapore, Singapore, 18th-22nd September 2023*, volume 3490 of *CEUR Workshop Proceedings*. CEUR-WS.org.

Jens-Joris Decorte, Jeroen Van Hautte, Johannes Deleu, Chris Develder, and Thomas Demeester. 2022. Design of negative sampling strategies for distantly supervised skill extraction. *arXiv preprint arXiv:2209.05987*.

Jens-Joris Decorte, Severine Verlinden, Jeroen Van Hautte, Johannes Deleu, Chris Develder, and Thomas Demeester. 2023. Extreme multi-label skill extraction training using large language models. *CoRR*, abs/2307.10778.

Jacob Devlin, Ming-Wei Chang, Kenton Lee, and Kristina Toutanova. 2019. BERT: Pre-training of deep bidirectional transformers for language understanding. In *Proceedings of the 2019 Conference of the North American Chapter of the Association for Computational Linguistics: Human Language Technologies, Volume 1 (Long and Short Papers)*, pages 4171–4186, Minneapolis, Minnesota. Association for Computational Linguistics.

Jiahui Gao, Renjie Pi, Lin Yong, Hang Xu, Jiacheng Ye, Zhiyong Wu, Weizhong Zhang, Xiaodan Liang, Zhenguo Li, and Lingpeng Kong. 2023. Self-guided noise-free data generation for efficient zero-shot learning. In *International Conference on Learning Representations (ICLR 2023)*.

Ann-sophie Gnehm, Eva Bühlmann, Helen Buchs, and Simon Clematide. 2022. Fine-grained extraction and classification of skill requirements in German-speaking job ads. In *Proceedings of the Fifth Workshop on Natural Language Processing and Computational Social Science (NLP+CSS)*, pages 14–24, Abu Dhabi, UAE. Association for Computational Linguistics.

Or Honovich, Thomas Scialom, Omer Levy, and Timo Schick. 2022. Unnatural instructions: Tuning language models with (almost) no human labor. *arXiv preprint arXiv:2212.09689*.

Varun Kumar, Ashutosh Choudhary, and Eunah Cho. 2020. Data augmentation using pre-trained transformer models. *arXiv preprint arXiv:2003.02245*.

Martin le Vrang, Agis Papantoniou, Erika Pauwels, Pieter Fannes, Dominique Vandensteen, and Johan De Smedt. 2014. Esco: Boosting job matching in europe with semantic interoperability. *Computer*, 47(10):57–64.

Vladimir I Levenshtein et al. 1966. Binary codes capable of correcting deletions, insertions, and reversals. In *Soviet physics doklady*, volume 10, pages 707–710. Soviet Union.

Jiachang Liu, Dinghan Shen, Yizhe Zhang, Bill Dolan, Lawrence Carin, and Weizhu Chen. 2022. What makes good in-context examples for GPT-3? In *Proceedings of Deep Learning Inside Out (DeeLIO 2022): The 3rd Workshop on Knowledge Extraction and Integration for Deep Learning Architectures*, pages 100–114, Dublin, Ireland and Online. Association for Computational Linguistics.

Aman Madaan, Niket Tandon, Prakhar Gupta, Skyler Hallinan, Luyu Gao, Sarah Wiegreffe, Uri Alon, Nouha Dziri, Shrimai Prabhumoye, Yiming Yang, Sean Welleck, Bodhisattwa Prasad Majumder, Shashank Gupta, Amir Yazdanbakhsh, and Peter Clark. 2023. Self-refine: Iterative refinement with self-feedback. *CoRR*, abs/2303.17651.

Sovesh Mohapatra and Somesh Mohapatra. 2022. Sentiment is all you need to win US presidential elections. In *Proceedings of the 2nd International Workshop on Natural Language Processing for Digital Humanities*, pages 15–20, Taipei, Taiwan. Association for Computational Linguistics.

OpenAI. 2023. GPT-3.5 Documentation. `https://platform.openai.com/docs/models`.

Alec Radford, Jeff Wu, Rewon Child, David Luan, Dario Amodei, and Ilya Sutskever. 2019. Language models are unsupervised multitask learners.

Nils Reimers and Iryna Gurevych. 2019. Sentence-BERT: Sentence embeddings using Siamese BERT-networks. In *Proceedings of the 2019 Conference on Empirical Methods in Natural Language Processing and the 9th International Joint Conference on Natural Language Processing (EMNLP-IJCNLP)*, pages 3982–3992, Hong Kong, China. Association for Computational Linguistics.

Zhihong Shao, Yeyun Gong, Yelong Shen, Minlie Huang, Nan Duan, and Weizhu Chen. 2023. Synthetic prompting: Generating chain-of-thought demonstrations for large language models. *arXiv preprint arXiv:2302.00618*.

Shuhe Wang, Xiaofei Sun, Xiaoya Li, Rongbin Ouyang, Fei Wu, Tianwei Zhang, Jiwei Li, and Guoyin Wang. 2023. Gpt-ner: Named entity recognition via large language models. *arXiv preprint arXiv:2304.10428*.

Zirui Wang, Adams Wei Yu, Orhan Firat, and Yuan Cao. 2021. Towards zero-label language learning. *arXiv preprint arXiv:2109.09193*.

Jiacheng Ye, Jiahui Gao, Qintong Li, Hang Xu, Jiangtao Feng, Zhiyong Wu, Tao Yu, and Lingpeng Kong. 2022. ZeroGen: Efficient zero-shot learning via dataset generation. In *Proceedings of the 2022 Conference on Empirical Methods in Natural Language Processing*, pages 11653–11669, Abu Dhabi, United Arab Emirates. Association for Computational Linguistics.

Mike Zhang, Kristian Jensen, Sif Sonniks, and Barbara Plank. 2022a. SkillSpan: Hard and soft skill extraction from English job postings. In *Proceedings of the 2022 Conference of the North American Chapter of the Association for Computational Linguistics: Human Language Technologies*, pages 4962–4984, Seattle, United States. Association for Computational Linguistics.

Mike Zhang, Kristian Nørgaard Jensen, and Barbara Plank. 2022b. Kompetencer: Fine-grained skill classification in Danish job postings via distant supervision and transfer learning. In *Proceedings of the Thirteenth Language Resources and Evaluation Conference*, pages 436–447, Marseille, France. European Language Resources Association.

A Prompts

A.1 Extraction Demonstrations

In our in-context learning pipeline, we provide seven demonstrations to guide the LLM in performing extractions. Below is one example.

Sentence: we are looking for a team leader with strong communication skills to foster collaboration and information sharing within the team.
Answer: We are looking for a team leader with strong @@communication skills## to foster collaboration and information sharing within the team.

Sentence: the ability to work collaboratively across disciplines is a key criterion for this position.
Answer: @@ability to collaborate across disciplines## is a key criterion for this position.

Sentence: As a Java Senior Software Engineer with experience, you will be a member of a Scrum team.
Answer: As a Java Senior Software Engineer with experience, you will be a member of a Scrum team.

Sentence: In her role as a team leader, she has continuously supported the professional development of her employees.
Answer: In her role as a team leader, she has continuously fostered the professional @@development of her employees##.

Sentence: He is a resilient employee who has been able to set proper priorities and organize tasks thoughtfully during periods of heavy workload.
Answer: He is a resilient employee who has been able to set @@correct priorities and organize tasks thoughtfully## during periods of high workload.

Sentence: Highly qualified, flexible employees from the insurance and IT industry develop them further.
Answer: Highly qualified, flexible employees from the insurance and IT industries continue to develop them.

Sentence: Over the past few years, it has succeeded in continuously

developing itself in a rapidly changing environment.
Answer: Over the past few years, he has succeeded in @@continuously developing## himself in a rapidly changing environment##.

A.2 Matching

A.2.1 Prompt

Here we provide the prompt used to match each extracted skill to one of the pre-selected candidates. The one-shot demonstration used in this prompt is provided in section A.2.2.

System: You are an expert human resource manager. You need to analyse skills in a job posting.

Instruction: You are given a sentence from a job description, and a skill extracted from this sentence. Choose from the list of options the one that best match the skill in the context. Answer with the associated letter.

{Demonstration}

Sentence: {Sentence}
Skills: {Extracted}
A: {Candidate 1}
...
J: {Candidate 10}

Answer:

A.2.2 Demonstration

The demonstration we use in the matching step (Section A.2.1) of our in-context learning pipeline.

Sentence: Understand basic provisions of copyright and privacy.
Skill: Data protection.
Options:
A: "Respect privacy principles"
B: "Understand data protection"
C: "Ensure data protection in aviation operations"
D: "Data protection"
Answer: b, d.

A.3 Generation of dataset

A.3.1 Positive samples

We use this prompt to generate samples containing ESCO skills.

System: You are the leading AI Writer at a large, multinational HR agency. You are considered as the world's best expert at expressing required skills and knowledge in a variety of clear ways. You are particularly proficient with the ESCO Occupation and Skills framework. As you are widely lauded for your job posting writing ability, you will assist the user in all job-posting, job requirements and occupational skills related tasks.

Instruction: You work in collaboration with ESCO to gather rigid standards for job postings. Given a list of ESCO skills and knowledges, you're asked to produce a single example of exactly one sentence that could be found in a job ad and refer to all skill or knowledge component. Ensure that your sentence is well written and could be found in real job advertisement. Use a variety of styles. You're trying to provide a representative sample of the many, many ways real job postings would evoke skills. All the skills in : {skillList} must be integrated. A candidate should have different degrees of expertise in all the given skills. This degree should be specified for each skills in the sentence. You must not include any skills in ESCO that were not given to you. Try to be as implicit as possible when mentionning the skill. Try not to use the exact skill string {wordsToAvoid}. Avoid explicitly using the wording of this extra information in your examples. Your sentence must not start with

'We are seeking', 'We are looking' or 'We are searching'. Generate stricly only one example.

A.3.2 Negative samples

We use two different prompts to generate negative samples: This first prompt generates negative samples that describe the company.

System: You are the leading AI Writer at a large, multinational HR agency. You are considered as the world's best expert at writing introductions of job posting.

Instruction: You are the leading AI Writer at a large, multinational HR agency. You are considered as the world's best expert at writing introductions of job posting. You should write {nExamples} examples of the first line of the job posting. It should consists in introducing the company, its localization, the number of employees, and any information relevant to a future candidates who wants to learn about the company. The description should be concise, specify the potential growth of the company and a domain of action. You shouldn't mentoin anything about the actual job, no skills required for the candidate and shouldn't mention the candidate at all. You should mention a wide range of company field, size, and localization in each of the examples.

This second prompt generates sentences detailing the salary and perks of a job.

System: You are the leading AI Writer at a large, multinational HR agency. You are considered as the world's best expert at specifying administrative information in job posting.

Instruction: You are the leading AI Writer at a large, multinational HR agency. You are considered as the world's best expert at specifying administrative information in job posting. You should produce {nExamples} descriptions of the salary and the perks a candidate to a certain job would have. You shouldn't mention the actual job and the candidate itself. You could add diversity by varying the salary and the perks. You must write a salary range between 40k and 100k according to the job in half of your generation.

A.4 Refinement of dataset

A.4.1 Initial prompt

System: You are an expert human resource manager. You need to analyse skills in a job posting.

Instruction: You are an expert human resource manager. You are given an extract from a job description and a skill coming from ESCO. Highlight all the parts of the job description that relates to the given skill, by surrounding them with tags '@@' at the beginning and '##' at the end. You should rewrite the entire sentence. The highlighted parts should precisely talk about the given skills and only this skills. The higlighted parts must precisely be about the given skills. Do not highlight parts not related to it. The sentence should be rewritten perfectly, using the same exact same words. You must highlight at least one part in the sentence that you will rewrite. The highlighted part should be as short as possible.

A.4.2 Refining shots

In case of incorrectly bound annotations :

In your response, you highlighted some parts using @@ at the beginning and @@ at the end.

```
Please use @@ at the beginning of the parts and ## at the end of the part you want to highlight. Annotate the previous sentence, but with the correct highlighting.
```

When there is a lack of annotations :

```
In your response, you highlighted nothing. Please annotate the previous sentence, and highlight at least one part linked to the skill.
```

B Ablation studies - Few-Shot ICL

B.1 Demonstrations

To conduct the experiments for the In-context Learning with LLM, we will use the demonstrations retrieval from the training set to provide few shots for both the extraction and the matching. We need to determine the number of demonstration to use for both parts. For this purpose we conduct an ablation study on SKILLSPAN-M 's validation test trying different configuration of number of shots. We try the following experiments :

- *baseline* : Same shots for all the sentences A.1 A.2.2
- M_1 : 1 demonstration for the matching part, baseline shot for extraction
- E_5 : 5 demonstration for the extraction part, baseline shot for matching
- E_7 : 7 demonstration for the extraction part, baseline shot for matching
- E_{10} : 10 demonstration for extraction, baseline shot for matching
- E_7M_1 : 1 demonstration for the matching part and 7 for the extraction part
- E_7M_3 : 3 demonstrations for the matching part and 7 for the extraction part

Given the stats in Table 4, displayed on Figure 2 we see the adding the demonstration retrieval for the extraction part yields a significative improvement on the recall. We will run the subsequent experiments with 7 demonstrations for the extraction part and one demonstration for the matching part.

	Recall	Precision	F_1
baseline	0.260	0.303	0.280
E_5	0.279	0.296	0.287
E_7	0.282	0.301	0.291
E_{10}	0.282	0.298	0.289
M_1	0.267	**0.305**	0.284
E_7M_1	**0.289**	0.298	**0.2934**
$E_{10}M_3$	0.283	0.293	0.288

Table 4: Ablation study for In-context Learning: Selecting optimal number of demonstrations for extraction and matching with GPT-3.5

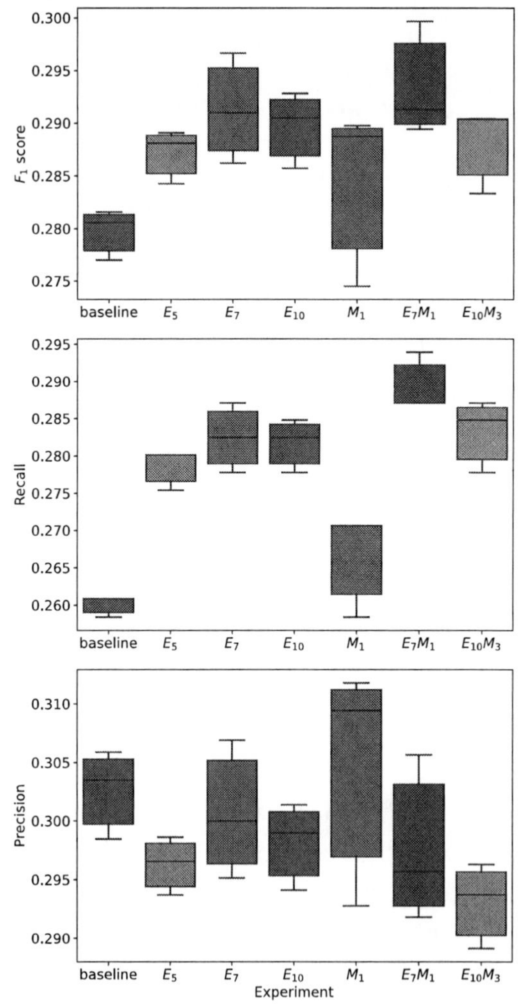

Figure 2: Ablation study for In-context Learning

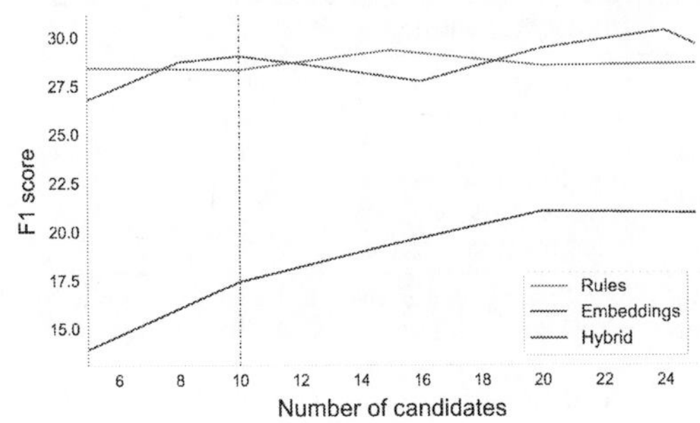

Figure 3: Rule-based, embedding-based, and hybrid candidate selection methods to select n candidates. Note, since the hybrid method takes the union of rule-based and embedding-based methods, $n = 5$ using the hybrid method would approximate $n \times 2$ actual number of actual candidates selected

# of Candidates	Precision	Recall	F_1
1	24.2	16.9	19.9
2	17.1	23.5	19.8

Table 5: Ablation study of the matching step: Performance of the ICL pipeline when taking only the top 1 or 2 candidates using the rule-based selection methods.

B.2 Candidate Selection

Figure 3 shows shows the F_1 scores of the ICL when we vary the number of candidates selected using the rule-based, embedding-based, and hybrid candidate selection methods, holding other elements constant. Looking at our results, we elect to use 10 candidates ($n = 5$) with the hybrid method.

While further increasing the candidates can increase matching performance slightly, we find that providing too many candidates can lead to a noticeable increase in inference time.

B.3 Matching Step

We conduct an ablation study on the matching. We remove the matching step from the pipeline and we only extract the spans from the inputted sentences and use rule-based to find matches. We focus on the rule-based method that yields the best results when extracting a small amount of candidates. Table 5 shows that the top-selected candidates are behind the performance of using GPT-3.5 as a reranker by around 8%. Therefore, we continue our experiments using the full three-step pipeline.

C Qualitative Analysis

We present various qualitative examples of predictions from the test set of SKILLSKAPE in Table 6. These examples include outcomes from both the supervised multi-label classifier and the in-context learning results using GPT-4. A key observation is the relatively lower number of skills predicted by the supervised classifier, which operates with a threshold of 0.15. Generally, these predictions are feasible and align closely with the gold standard label. However, it should be noted that the evaluation process tends to penalize these predictions for their limited scope.

D Other Summary Statistics on SKILLSKAPE

D.0.1 Skill Groups

We show in Table 7 the skill groups and counts of skills in each ESCO skill group that is included in the label spaced used for the SKILLSKAPE dataset.

D.0.2 Sentence Length

Looking at Figure 4, we can see that SKILLSKAPE has longer sentences and contains more variation in sentence length than DECORTE. The distribution of SKILLSKAPE resembles more that of real-world data (SKILLSPAN-M).

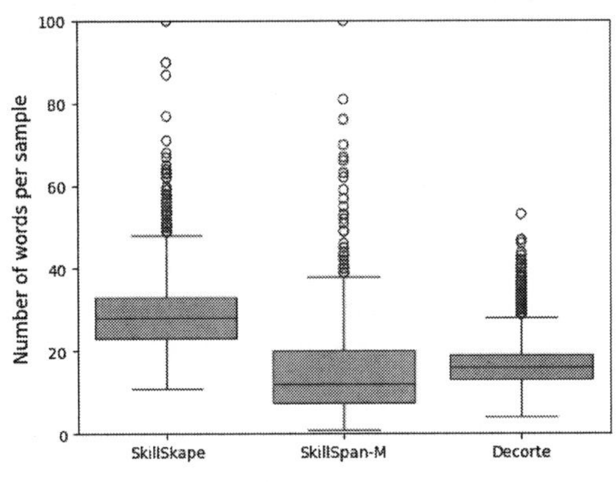

Figure 4: Sentence length distribution in the three datasets. SKILLSKAPE has much longer sentences. DECORTE has very short sentences and low length variance.

Sentence	Multi-label Classifier	In-context Learning	Gold
(1) Seeking a highly skilled individual with extensive expertise in overseeing and optimizing the operation and maintenance of various technical components and systems on board maritime vessels.	shipping industry	overseeing and optimizing the operation and maintenance of various technical components and systems on board maritime vessels	manage vessel engines and systems
(2) As an integral part of our team, the ideal candidate should possess a deep understanding of coordinating the alignment and seamless interaction of various system components, while executing rigorous testing and implementing an overarching strategy for the integration of ICT systems	ICT system integration, define integration strategy	coordinating the alignment and seamless interaction of various system components, rigorous testing, integration of ICT systems	ICT system integration, define integration strategy, define software architecture, manage ICT data architecture
(3) Ability to effectively adapt to changing circumstances while maintaining a vigilant attitude, maintaining composure in challenging situations, and efficiently managing workload and responsibilities.	handle stressful situations	effectively adapt to changing circumstances, vigilant attitude, composure, efficiently managing workload and responsibilities	exercise patience, adjust priorities, stay alert
(4) Are you an experienced professional with a proven track record in designing and implementing comprehensive technology testing frameworks, ensuring the seamless integration of software applications and systems?	develop ICT test suite, execute software tests	designing and implementing comprehensive technology testing frameworks, seamless integration of software applications and systems	develop ICT test suite

Table 6: We show several qualitative examples of predictions on the test set of SKILLSKAPE using the supervised multi-label classifier and in-context learning results with GPT-4.

Skill Group	skill count
agriculture, forestry, fisheries and veterinary	4
arts and humanities	8
assisting and caring	13
business, administration and law	40
communication, collaboration and creativity	111
constructing	3
education	3
engineering, manufacturing and construction	22
generic programmes and qualifications	6
handling and moving	15
health and welfare	7
information and communication technologies (icts)	71
information skills	57
management skills	65
natural sciences, mathematics and statistics	10
services	5
social sciences, journalism and information	1
working with computers	35
working with machinery and specialised equipment	14
TOTAL	514

Table 7: ESCO skill groups present in SKILLSKAPE dataset

HR-MultiWOZ: A Task Oriented Dialogue (TOD) Dataset for HR LLM Agent

Weijie Xu[1], **Zicheng Huang**[1], **Wenxiang Hu**[1], **Xi Fang**[1], **Rajesh Kumar Cherukuri**[1], **Naumaan Nayyar**[1], **Lorenzo Malandri**[2], **Srinivasan H. Sengamedu**[1]

[1]Amazon

[2]University of Milano-Bicocca

weijiexu@amazon.com

Abstract

Recent advancements in Large Language Models (LLMs) have been reshaping Natural Language Processing (NLP) task in several domains. Their use in the field of Human Resources (HR) has still room for expansions and could be beneficial for several time consuming tasks. Examples such as time-off submissions, medical claims filing, and access requests are noteworthy, but they are by no means the sole instances. However the aforementioned developments must grapple with the pivotal challenge of constructing a high-quality training dataset. On one hand, most conversation datasets are solving problems for customers not employees. On the other hand, gathering conversations with HR could raise privacy concerns. To solve it, we introduce HR-Multiwoz, a fully-labeled dataset of 550 conversations spanning 10 HR domains. Our work has the following contributions: (1) It is the first labeled open-sourced conversation dataset in the HR domain for NLP research. (2) It provides a detailed recipe for the data generation procedure along with data analysis and human evaluations. The data generation pipeline is transferable and can be easily adapted for labeled conversation data generation in other domains. (3) The proposed data-collection pipeline is mostly based on LLMs with minimal human involvement for annotation, which is time and cost-efficient.

1 Introduction

Recent advances in natural language processing (NLP) have been applied in a variety of tasks in the Human Resources (HR) domain ranging from skill extraction (Zhang et al., 2022), job understanding (Decorte et al., 2021) to candidate sourcing (Hemamou and Coleman, 2022). Unlike NLP research in other domains (Zhao et al., 2021a,b), numerous HR processes remain highly inefficient, such as requesting time off, scheduling meetings, submitting tickets for IT issues, or filing medical claims. In fact, the Asana Work Index report shows that knowledge workers spend 60 percent of their time on repetitive work.

LLM agent (Gao et al., 2023) uses LLMs as its central computational engine, allowing it to carry on conversations, do tasks, reason, and display a degree of autonomy. Similar to other domains (Kalvakurthi et al., 2023; Hsu et al., 2023), creating an LLM agent to help with these tasks could save a significant amount of time for employees and improve job satisfaction. A good LLM agent should be able to understand the requirements of users (Liu et al., 2023). The ideal dataset to evaluate or train an HR LLM agent should contain conversations between a virtual assistant and employees, annotated with dialogue states. Dialogue states contain representations of a conversation's current context such as intentions and relevant information.

For a dataset to be useful in building/evaluating an HR LLM agent, it must satisfy the following four requirements: (1) The information in the dialogue state must be **extractive**. When using an LLM agent to file a medical claim, employees must be able to trust that the system will accurately retrieve the right number. Thus, the extracted information must be from the conversation. (2) The information in the dialogue state should contain **long entity**. When using a LLM agent to solve a code bug, employees have to provide more detail about the code issue. This means that the extracted information should be long enough to give the LLM agent correct information. (3) The dataset must be **HR specific** and discuss about HR-relevant tasks. (4) The conversation must be **empathetic**. In real conversations with HR, it is important to communicate with employees respectfully. This could enhance inclusive culture within the organization. The LLM agent built on this dataset could also be empathetic.

There are many open-source conversation

Proceedings of the First Workshop on Natural Language Processing for Human Resources (NLP4HR 2024), pages 59–72

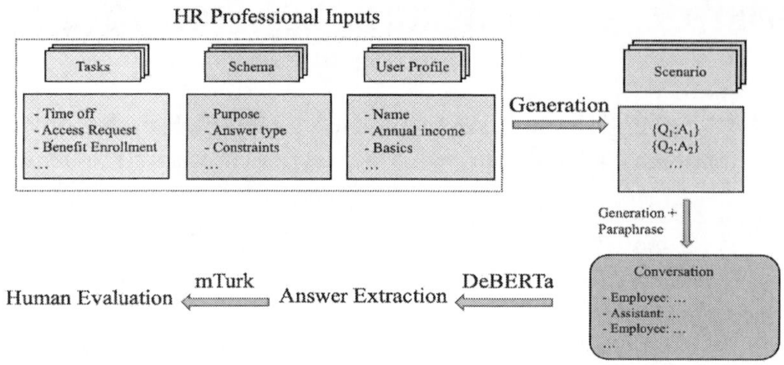

Figure 1: The figure describes the data generation pipeline. The HR experts start by identifying tasks, creating schemas, and generating employee profiles. LLM is applied to generate diverse scenarios and paraphrase to make the conversation more natural. The label is then extracted by DeBERTa and refined by MTurk.

datasets. Schema-Guided Dialogue (SGD) (Rastogi et al., 2020) is a dialogue dataset with evolving ontologies, introducing new test set slots and services, emphasizing DST performance and zero-shot generalization. SGD-X (Lee et al., 2022) expands on SGD, presenting five additional schema styles. M2M (Shah et al., 2018) connects a developer, who provides the task-specific information, and a framework, which provides the task-independent information, for generating dialogues centered around completing the task. MultiWOZ (Budzianowski et al., 2020) features human-human dialogues using a stable ontology. However, all these datasets *are customer-facing instead of employee-facing.* Also, *none of them is fully extractive or related to HR. The extracted information is also short in size.* HR LLM agent trained on these models may not be empathetic, extract complete information from employees and misunderstand employees' intent. Thus, it is essential to create a new dataset for HR application. On the other hand, collecting real datasets is difficult because the company cannot share these conversations with the public as it could leak employee confidential information.

In response, we create an HR domain-specific dataset for LLM HR Agent. It is extractive, contains a long entity, is HR-specific, and contains empathetic conversations. We summarize our contributions as follows:

- We've designed a data generation recipe that is efficient, cost-effective, high quality, and domain-specific. The same recipe can be easily adapted for labeled conversation generation in other domains.
- We created a dataset of size 550 specifically for 10 HR use cases. The information in the dialogue state is extractive and contains a long entity.
- The generated conversations are natural, clear, and empathetic based on human evaluations. The conversation is more comprehensive, detailed, richer in content, and diverse compared to existing datasets.

2 Methods

Our proposed data generation method is inspired by MultiWOZ (Budzianowski et al., 2020). In Multiwoz, two annotators played the roles of a user and a wizard. The user was given a specific goal in a certain domain (like booking a hotel), and the wizard, having access to a database, responded to the user's requests. However, it requires a lot of human labeling which is expensive. With recent advancements of LLMs (Brown et al., 2020), we can use LLMs to replace humans in generating more diverse scenarios and rephrasing conversations. At a high level, our generation process includes developing expert-validated HR schemas, generating diverse user profiles, creating realistic scenarios via Claude, randomizing and merging, rephrasing dialogues using Claude, and applying extractive modeling using DeBERTa model (He et al., 2021) and human labeling to get high-quality labels. We chose Claude because of cost and ethical reasons as explained in Appendix G. For each step, we provide detailed instructions and human labeling guidance in the Appendix. **This makes our data genera-**

tion method easily transferable, reproducible and transparent. It took 2 days and costed 38.32 dollars for LLMs inference and 49.82 dollars for Human labeling. **This makes our method time and cost effective.** The detailed data generation pipeline is in Fig 1 and a provided example is in Fig 2.

Schema Creation The input of the system includes diverse task schemas for different HR-related tasks. Each schema is composed of a series of structured questions, the schema's purpose, answer type, and constraints for each potential value. To ensure domain relevance and accuracy, these task schemas undergo a thorough audit by HR domain experts. The domain includes benefits enrollment, performance review, training requirements, safety incident report, relocation request, harassment report, goal setting, access request, it issues report and time off report. Each schema contains different slots. **This makes our generated dataset HR Specific.** For each slot, we also designed a question, answer type, and potential choices. The detailed example of task schema is in Table 2.

Next, we develop a user profile schema, focusing on the user's preference. This user profile schema aims to maximize diversity and represent a wide range of real-world scenarios. An example profile includes attributes such as Number of Dependents, Contact Preference, Annual Income, etc. These user profile schema were generated by Claude. We manually remove user profiles that share more than 2 entries with other profiles to maximize the diversity. A detailed example of a user profile is in Table 3. For company specific schema and user profile, company can adapt the same logic and modify the key and value to be company specific.

Scenario Generation The scenario is the outline of the conversation. Taking the user profile and task schemas as input, we generate a realistic template as a Python dictionary (Question as key and generated answer from the selected user profile as value). We first complete the answer from the selected task schema using the user profile. Secondly, Claude is employed to answer the rest of the question in the scenario from the user's perspective. We instruct LLM to ensure that answers are concise yet informative. The detailed prompt is in Table 4.

Conversation Generation and Paraphrasing To transform a scenario into a conversation, it should adopt a natural tone and structure. For instance, the conversation should be empathetic and includes expressions like "Cool", "Okay" etc. Also, in a real-world conversation, a user can sometimes answer multiple questions in one turn. For each template, we then randomize the order of the scenario. We randomly combine answers of similar types into a single response. We then rewrite it as a question and answer. Finally, we use LLM to paraphrase questions and answers to enhance empathy in the questions and naturalness and completeness in responses. This paraphrase also provides a long entity such as a detailed description of a code error. Thus, **the paraphrased conversations are empathetic and the information in dialogue states contains long entity** The detailed prompt is in Table 5.

Dialogue States Labeling The quality of the generated dialogues was assessed through answer extraction, data cleaning, and human evaluation. The answer was extracted using DeBERTa (He et al., 2021) from the generated dialogues. This model is chosen for its compact size, effectiveness in extraction tasks, and capability to provide confidence scores between 0 and 1. We input questions, ground truth answers, and context into the model to extract answers with corresponding confidence levels. This step is crucial to ensure that answers in our dataset are not only informative but also extractable with a degree of certainty, which makes it easier to identify wrong answers. **This step makes the information in dialogue states extractive.**

The extracted answers were cleaned for use in the TOD system through a series of steps. We first remove all leading and trailing spaces, which often occurs as a byproduct of extraction processes. To align with the format of answers in the conversation template, we also remove all trailing punctuation marks. This step eliminates ambiguities and preserves the integrity.

We further use mechanical turk to verify if the formatted extracted answer is equivalent to the answer in the scenario as asking a question in Figure 3. Following (Li et al., 2023), we selected the extracted answer with confidence below 0.1 for Mechanical Turk. This contains 692 data points. The answer can only be yes or no. We use 3 labelers per task and pay them 0.024 per task. If the response is 'no', we further label the data manually by HR professionals. Out of 71 data points marked as 'no', HR professionals identified 27 as inaccurately labeled and corrected them with the correct answer that is extractable from the conversation.

3 Evaluation

Dataset Statistics: We are releasing the HR Multiwoz dataset comprising a total of 550 dialogues collected using the proposed method in Sec. 2. This dataset covers HR-related tasks including benefits enrollment, performance review, training requirements, safety incident reports, relocation requests, harassment reports, goal settings, access requests, IT issues reporting, and time off reports as shown in Table. 6. Our dataset covers diverse topics in HR and provides a wide range of examples. Thus, compared to the existing dataset, we recommend using this dataset for transfer learning tasks in other HR-related use cases.

Datasets Comparison: Compared to the existed dataset, the HR Multiwoz dataset exhibits diversity and completeness in questions and answers, as illustrated in Table 1. The dataset contains fewer dialogues than the M2M restaurant dataset, yet it surpasses it in total turns and total tokens. **This indicates that the HR Multiwoz dialogues are extended and richer in content.** HR Multiwoz achieves the highest average turns per dialogue and average tokens per turn. This suggests that **the conversations are both comprehensive and detailed.**

Furthermore, the highest ratios of unique tokens and unique bigrams in our dataset signify a broader verbal crucial for natural responses. Such diversity in language use is indicative of the dataset's capacity to simulate real-world conversations in the HR-specific domain. Additionally, **the inclusion of long entities in user answers, as suggested by the highest average tokens per answer**, enhances the dataset's utility for training sophisticated dialogue systems that require an understanding of extended contexts and nuanced language. Overall, the HR Multiwoz dataset appears to be well-suited for developing/evaluating HR LLM Agents that can effectively handle empathetic, natural, and complete interactions in HR-specific scenarios.

Human Evaluations: In the subjective evaluation of the Multiwoz dataset, crowd workers assessed the naturalness of employees' responses, the clarity of HR's questions, and the politeness of HR's questions. For each category, only responses with confidence scores above 60 percent were considered, resulting in 634 employee answers, 623 HR questions for clarity, and 629 HR questions for politeness in the evaluation set. Statistical analysis using one-sample t-tests revealed that the average ratings for employees' naturalness, HR's question clarity, and HR's question politeness were significantly higher than neutral. This was evidenced by high t-statistics (19.31 for naturalness, 18.83 for clarity, and 16.02 for politeness) and extremely low p-values, indicating **strong positive ratings in the naturalness of employees' responses, the clarity of HR's questions, and the politeness of HR's questions.** The detailed score distributions, instructions and detailed analysis are in Appendix K, Appendix L and Appendix E.

Metrics	multiwoz	M2MR	ours
Dialogues	8437	1116	550
Total turns	113552	6188	8910
Total tokens	1742157	99932	181363
Avg. turns per dialogue	13.46	11.09	**16.2**
Avg. tokens per turn	15.34	8.07	**20.35**
Avg. tokens per answer	13.46	5.56	**14.53**
Unique tokens / Total tokens	0.0103	0.0092	**0.0156**
Unique bigrams / Total tokens	0.0634	0.0670	**0.1177**

Table 1: Comparing Multiwoz 2.2, M2M Restaurants and our datasets: HR-MultiWOZ on diversity of language and dialogue flows.

4 Conclusions

HR-Multiwoz, our generated dataset of 550 labeled conversations, can evaluate/train HR LLM agents by offering 10 domain-specific, diverse, comprehensive, detailed labeled conversations. Our data generation approach minimizes human annotation efforts while maximizing data relevance and quality, leveraging Claude. This makes our data generation approach transferable. As the first dataset in HR dialogue systems, HR-Multiwoz represents a significant advancement in HR automation, providing rich and empathetic dialogues ideal for training efficient, human-like HR digital assistants. It satisfies all HR dialogue requirements and sets a new benchmark for HR applications, paving the way for innovative, AI-driven HR solutions. In the future, we suggest to enhance this dataset by increasing the number of conversations, extending to other languages beyond English, and including suggest API to call at the end of each conversation. We will use cc-by-4.0 license. We provide ethical statement and limitations in Appendix A and Appendix B

References

Tom B. Brown, Benjamin Mann, Nick Ryder, Melanie Subbiah, Jared Kaplan, Prafulla Dhariwal, Arvind Neelakantan, Pranav Shyam, Girish Sastry, Amanda Askell, Sandhini Agarwal, Ariel Herbert-Voss, Gretchen Krueger, Tom Henighan, Rewon Child, Aditya Ramesh, Daniel M. Ziegler, Jeffrey Wu, Clemens Winter, Christopher Hesse, Mark Chen, Eric Sigler, Mateusz Litwin, Scott Gray, Benjamin Chess, Jack Clark, Christopher Berner, Sam McCandlish, Alec Radford, Ilya Sutskever, and Dario Amodei. 2020. Language models are few-shot learners.

Paweł Budzianowski, Tsung-Hsien Wen, Bo-Hsiang Tseng, Iñigo Casanueva, Stefan Ultes, Osman Ramadan, and Milica Gašić. 2020. Multiwoz – a large-scale multi-domain wizard-of-oz dataset for task-oriented dialogue modelling.

Jens-Joris Decorte, Jeroen Van Hautte, Thomas Demeester, and Chris Develder. 2021. Jobbert: Understanding job titles through skills.

Chen Gao, Xiaochong Lan, Nian Li, Yuan Yuan, Jingtao Ding, Zhilun Zhou, Fengli Xu, and Yong Li. 2023. Large language models empowered agent-based modeling and simulation: A survey and perspectives. *arXiv preprint arXiv:2312.11970.*

Pengcheng He, Xiaodong Liu, Jianfeng Gao, and Weizhu Chen. 2021. Deberta: Decoding-enhanced bert with disentangled attention.

Leo Hemamou and William Coleman. 2022. Delivering fairness in human resources AI: Mutual information to the rescue. In *Proceedings of the 2nd Conference of the Asia-Pacific Chapter of the Association for Computational Linguistics and the 12th International Joint Conference on Natural Language Processing (Volume 1: Long Papers)*, pages 867–882, Online only. Association for Computational Linguistics.

Shang-Ling Hsu, Raj Sanjay Shah, Prathik Senthil, Zahra Ashktorab, Casey Dugan, Werner Geyer, and Diyi Yang. 2023. Helping the helper: Supporting peer counselors via ai-empowered practice and feedback.

Vishesh Kalvakurthi, Aparna S. Varde, and John Jenq. 2023. Hey dona! can you help me with student course registration?

Harrison Lee, Raghav Gupta, Abhinav Rastogi, Yuan Cao, Bin Zhang, and Yonghui Wu. 2022. SGD-x: A benchmark for robust generalization in schema-guided dialogue systems. *Proceedings of the AAAI Conference on Artificial Intelligence*, 36(10):10938–10946.

Minzhi Li, Taiwei Shi, Caleb Ziems, Min-Yen Kan, Nancy Chen, Zhengyuan Liu, and Diyi Yang. 2023. CoAnnotating: Uncertainty-guided work allocation between human and large language models for data annotation. In *Proceedings of the 2023 Conference on Empirical Methods in Natural Language Processing*, pages 1487–1505, Singapore. Association for Computational Linguistics.

Xiao Liu, Hao Yu, Hanchen Zhang, Yifan Xu, Xuanyu Lei, Hanyu Lai, Yu Gu, Hangliang Ding, Kaiwen Men, Kejuan Yang, Shudan Zhang, Xiang Deng, Aohan Zeng, Zhengxiao Du, Chenhui Zhang, Sheng Shen, Tianjun Zhang, Yu Su, Huan Sun, Minlie Huang, Yuxiao Dong, and Jie Tang. 2023. Agentbench: Evaluating llms as agents.

Abhinav Rastogi, Xiaoxue Zang, Srinivas Sunkara, Raghav Gupta, and Pranav Khaitan. 2020. Towards scalable multi-domain conversational agents: The schema-guided dialogue dataset.

Pararth Shah, Dilek Hakkani-Tür, Gokhan Tür, Abhinav Rastogi, Ankur Bapna, Neha Nayak, and Larry Heck. 2018. Building a conversational agent overnight with dialogue self-play.

Weijie Xu, Wenxiang Hu, Fanyou Wu, and Srinivasan Sengamedu. 2023a. DeTiME: Diffusion-enhanced topic modeling using encoder-decoder based LLM. In *Findings of the Association for Computational Linguistics: EMNLP 2023*, pages 9040–9057, Singapore. Association for Computational Linguistics.

Weijie Xu, Xiaoyu Jiang, Srinivasan Sengamedu Hanumantha Rao, Francis Iannacci, and Jinjin Zhao. 2023b. vONTSS: vMF based semi-supervised neural topic modeling with optimal transport. In *Findings of the Association for Computational Linguistics: ACL 2023*, pages 4433–4457, Toronto, Canada. Association for Computational Linguistics.

Weijie Xu, Jinjin Zhao, Francis Iannacci, and Bo Wang. 2021. Ffpdg: Fast, fair and private data generation. In *ICLR 2021 Workshop on Synthetic Data Generation.*

Mike Zhang, Kristian Jensen, Sif Sonniks, and Barbara Plank. 2022. Skillspan: Hard and soft skill extraction from english job postings. In *Proceedings of the 2022 Conference of the North American Chapter of the Association for Computational Linguistics: Human Language Technologies*, pages 4962–4984.

Jinjin Zhao, Kim Larson, Weijie Xu, Neelesh Gattani, and Candace Thille. 2021a. Targeted feedback generation for constructed-response questions. In *AAAI 2021 Workshop on AI Education.*

Jinjin Zhao, Weijie Xu, and Candace Thille. 2021b. End-to-end question generation to assist formative assessment design for conceptual knowledge learning. In *AETS 2021*.

A Ethics Statement

Ethics Statement The dataset generated by AI in the HR space necessitates careful consideration of ethical issues related to safety, privacy, and bias. There is a possibility that, in attempting to assist, AI generated dataset may cause more harm than benefit. In response, in collaboration with security reviewer and HR professionals, we have taken the following steps in order to minimize the risks of harm.

Human Labeling: To make sure the generated conversation is polite and empathetic, we use human labelers to label the conversation.

Guardrail: We remove conversation that is labeled by human that contains rude language. This makes sure the language is not rude.

Privacy: In our generated data, we use synthetic user profile which is not real. We also make sure the data in the system is in compliance with rigorous internal infoSec policies and standards.

Negative Examples/Potential Bias: To mitigate potential biases in generative models, we have employed an extractive approach. None the less, the effectiveness of extractions could vary with the employee's language fluency. This variation could potentially lead to inefficiencies in the Task-Oriented Dialogue (TOD) system for non-native English speakers. Efforts are underway to understand and address these issues.

Synthetic Data Bias: The dataset primarily relies on conversations generated through large language models (LLMs) and human rephrasing. This may introduce biases inherent in the LLMs or limit the scenarios to the creative constraints of the model's training data.

Limited Cultural and Linguistic Diversity: HR-Multiwoz may primarily reflect the cultural and linguistic norms of the data creators or the LLM training data. This limitation could affect the dataset's effectiveness in global or culturally diverse HR settings.

B Limitations

Updating and expanding the dataset to include new HR domains or to adapt to evolving HR practices and policies might require some efforts, given the reliance on new schema creation. The dataset does not contains task part of the conversation. This limits the use of this dataset to train an LLM agent to leverage different tools. This dataset also lacks evaluations on existed TOD systems method.

DeBERTa model also has some limitations. We observe additional complexities when comparing the original short answers with those extracted by DeBERTa, for example: (i) duplication of answers in a single turn containing multiple short answers, (ii) inclusion of prompting text like "Employee:", (iii) failure to extract meaningful answers or labels.

The performance of generated datasets is not fully controllable. human feedback is essential to further improve the dataset. With this regards, LLMs allow the user to be informed with the final outcome of the system (you have been assigned a time-off period from. . . to. . .) and check the correctness of the process.

C Future Work

Real-World Integration and Testing: Implementing the model trained on this dataset in real-world HR environments to test and refine its efficacy. This could include pilot programs with HR departments to gather feedback and improve the dataset's realism and applicability.

Cross-Cultural and Multilingual Expansion: Enhancing the dataset to include a broader range of cultural contexts and languages, making it more inclusive and applicable globally, especially in diverse workplaces.

Continuous Updating and Expansion: Regularly updating the dataset to reflect the latest HR practices, policies, and regulations. This could involve creating a framework for continuous data collection and integration.

Bias Detection and Mitigation: Implementing systematic methods to identify and mitigate biases in the dataset, ensuring fair and unbiased HR-related dialogues.

Broader Domain Generalization: Extending the dataset or its methodology to other domains beyond HR, thereby testing its adaptability and utility in various fields like customer service, healthcare, or legal advice.

User Experience Research: Conducting user experience research to understand how employees and HR professionals interact with AI-based systems trained on the dataset, aiming to improve user satisfaction and effectiveness.

Topic Modeling: Leveraging topic modeling

techniques to understand the theme in these conversations. (Xu et al., 2023b,a)

Differentially Private Dataset: Make sure dataset is fair and privacy preserving. (Xu et al., 2021)

D Task Profile

E Human Evaluation Analysis

For a subjective evaluation of the Multiwoz dataset, we want to understand the following: 1. Is the employees' answer natural? 2. Is the HR's question clear? 3. Is the HR's question polite or empathetic? We presented final dialogues to crowd workers, who rated each user and HR turn on a scale of 1 to 5 for the specific dimensions with 1 being very robotic and 5 being very natural. We sampled 650 turns from HR and employees to create the evaluation set. Each turn was shown to 3 crowd workers. We pay them 0.012 per task. Each answer also has a confidence score between 0 to 1, indicating the labelers' confidence in their assessment.

For question 1, we included data with confidence score larger than 60, resulting in 634 HR turns to create the evaluation set. Using a one-sample t-test, we showed that the average rating is significantly better than neutral indicating that the question from the employee's answer is natural (t-statistic around 19.31, p value ≤ 0.000000001.

For question 2, We only select confidence score larger than 60 which is 623 turn from HR to create the evaluation set. Score 3 is neutral. Score 5 is very clear. 1 is very unclear. The one-sample t-test to evaluate if the average is significantly better than neutral. The test gives a t-statistic of approximately 18.83 and an extremely small p-value (p value $\leq$ 0.000000001). This result indicates that the average rating is significantly better than neutral indicating that the question from HR is clear.

For question 3, We only select confidence score larger than 60 which is 629 turn from HR to create the evaluation set. Score 3 is neutral. Score 5 is very polite. 1 is very rude. The one-sample t-test to evaluate if the average is significantly better than neutral. The test gives a t-statistic of approximately 16.02 and an extremely small p-value (p value $\leq$ 0.000000001). This result indicates that the average rating is significantly better than neutral indicating that the question from HR is polite.

F Example of Data Generation Process

G Claude

We choose claude over GPT4 for the following reasons: **Cost Effiency**: Claude is more cost-effective in terms of computing resources required for data generation. For instance, using the GPT-4 8K context model via OpenAI's API costs \$0.03 for every 1K input tokens and \$0.06 for every 1K output tokens. **Data Privacy and Security** Claude offers better data privacy and security features, especially for sensitive tasks like generating data for HR-related applications. **Model Characteristics** Claude is trained RLAIF which could produce more ethical conversations.

H Generated Dataset Statistics

I Example of Generated Dialogues

J Answer Evaluation

K Human Evaluation Score Distribution

L Human Evaluation Instructions

Key	Description
type_of_benefit	What type of benefit do you want to enroll in? (e.g., Health Insurance, Dental Insurance, etc.)
benefit_plan_selection	Select your benefit plan by entering the plan code (e.g., Plan A, Plan B, etc.).
number_of_dependents	How many dependents do you want to add to the plan? (Enter a number)
previous_coverage_duration	How many years have you been previously covered under a health plan? (Enter a number)
effective_date	When do you want the coverage to start? (Enter the date in YYYY-MM-DD format)
personal_information_confirmation	Do we have your updated personal information on file? (Answer with Yes or No)
contact_preference	Please enter your preferred contact method (Email, Phone, Mail).
estimated_annual_premium	What is your estimated annual premium budget in USD? (Enter a number)

Table 2: Benefits Enrollment Schema Example. This is just an example. Each question could involve multiple types.

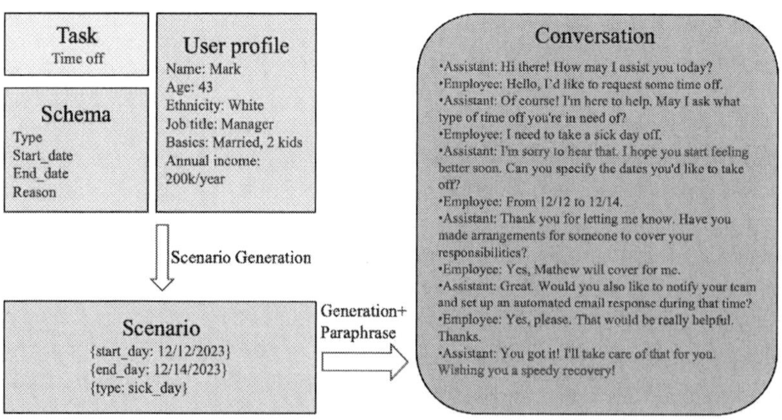

Figure 2: The figure describes a conversation generation process. We first identify task, schema and employee profile. We then use LLM to fill out the value in the schema. We then use LLM to rephrase the conversation to be more natural. We highlight the part that HR assistant show empathy in red.

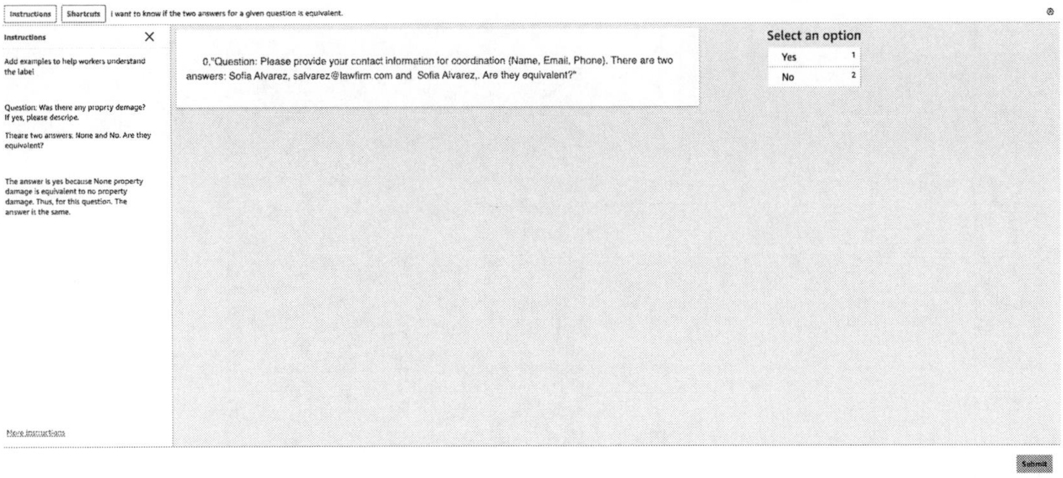

Figure 3: MTurk Questions and selected examples to understand if extracted answer is equivalent to the ground truth

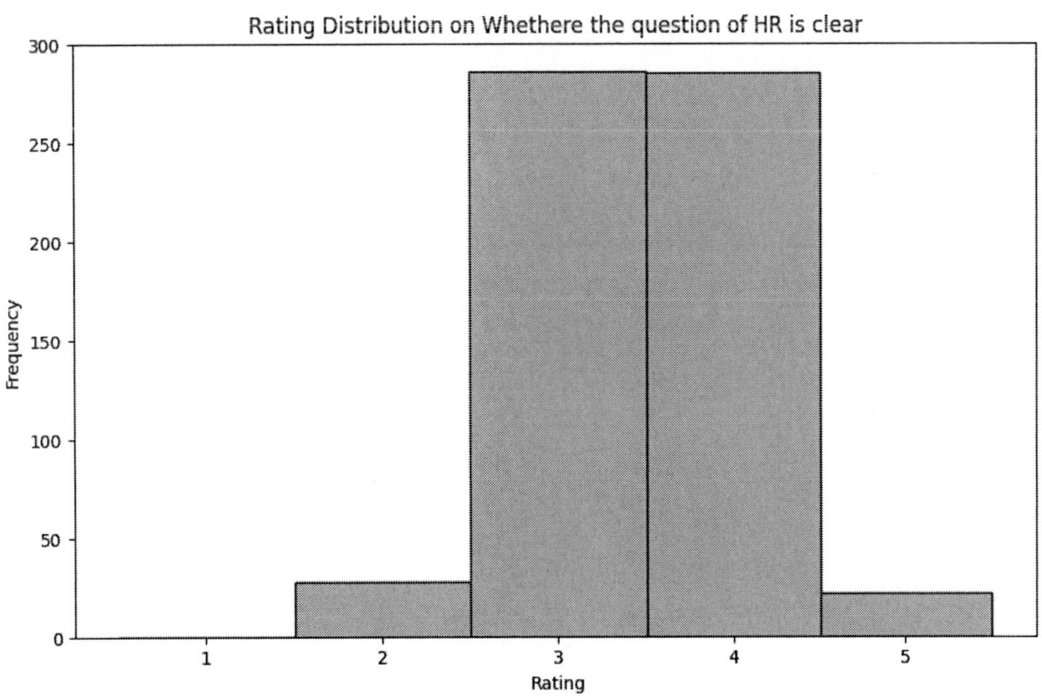

Figure 4: MTurk Score Distribution to understand if the HR question is clear

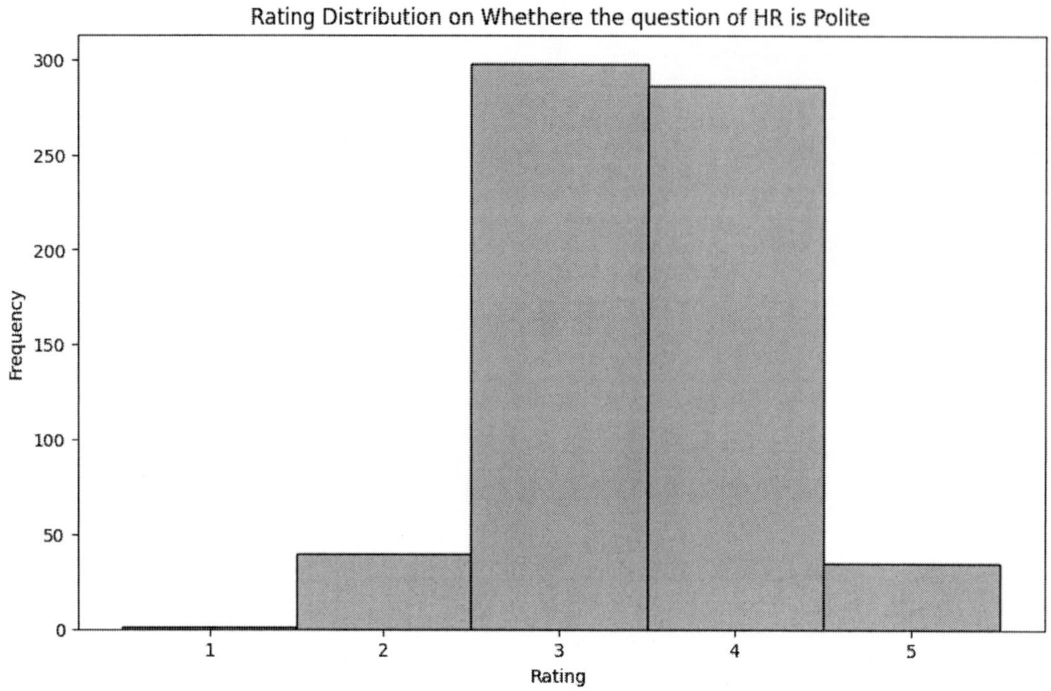

Figure 5: MTurk Score Distribution to understand if the HR question is polite

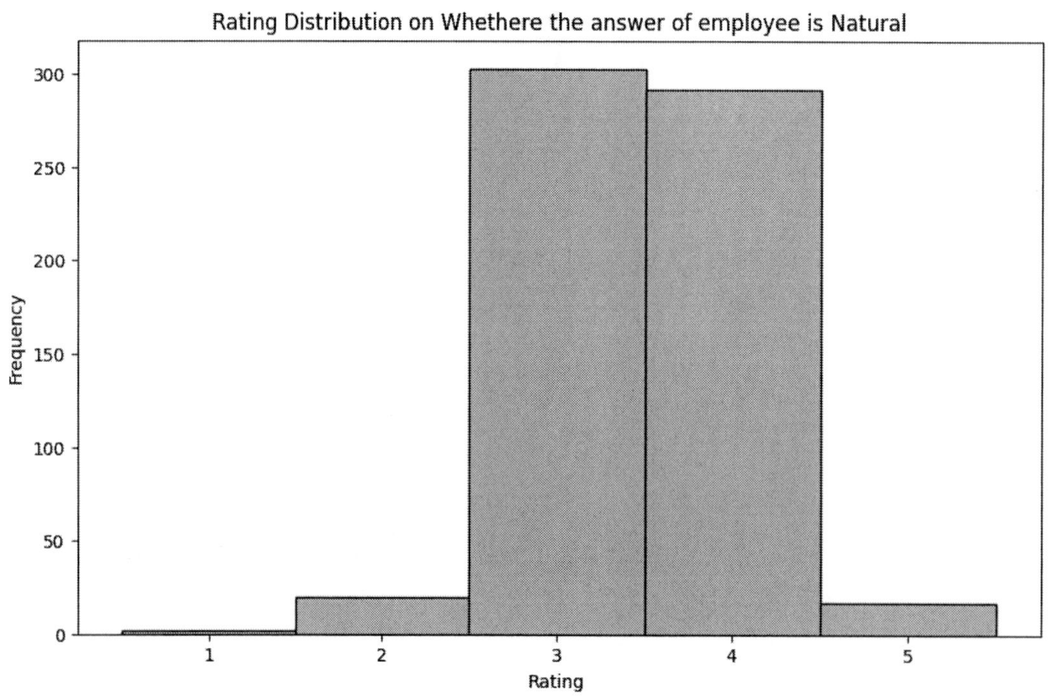

Figure 6: MTurk Score Distribution to understand if the employee answer is natural

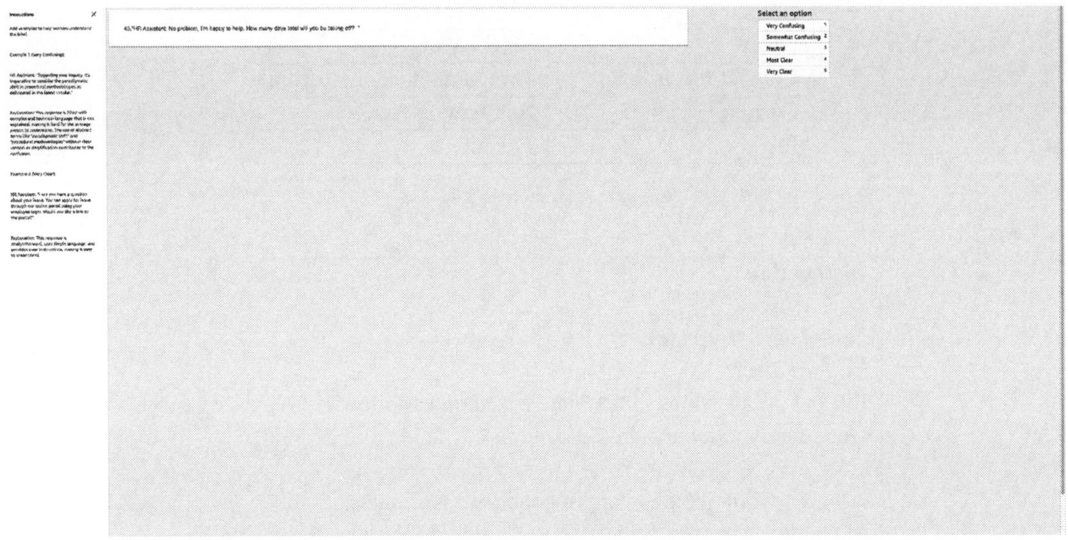

Figure 7: MTurk human instructions to understand if the HR question is clear

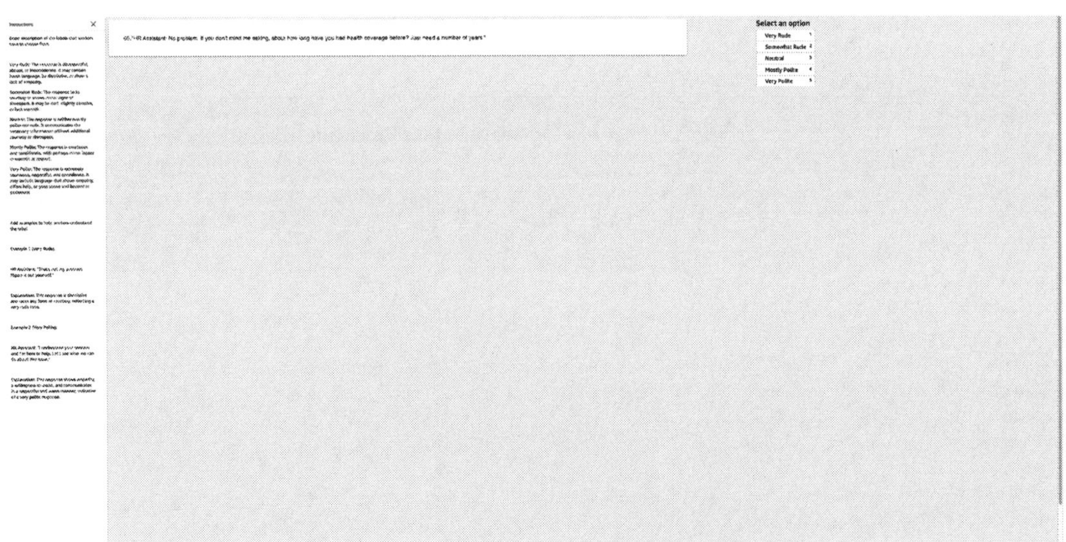

Figure 8: MTurk human instructions to understand if the HR question is polite

Key	Value
Number of Dependents	2
Contact Preference	Email
Annual Income	$150,000
Name	Dr. Li Wei
Contact Information	liwei@medicalemail.com
Current Location	San Francisco, CA
Job	Doctor

Table 3: User Profile Example

Instruction
User: {user} Template: {template} You are User. Fill out all questions in template based on experience. Generated dictionary should contain key name and generated answer. All keys from Template are in generated dictionary. Make the answer extremely short (within 5 words). Put the generated dictionary in <answer></answer>XML tags.

Table 4: Instructions for Template Generation

Instruction
Conversation: {conversation} This is the conversation between HR Assistant and an employee. 1. For each Question, paraphrase the question to make it more conversational by using more modal words and empathetic. 2. For each Answer, write it as a complete sentence. Please put the updated Conversation based on Template in <answer></answer>XML tags.

Table 5: Instructions for Conversation Rewriting

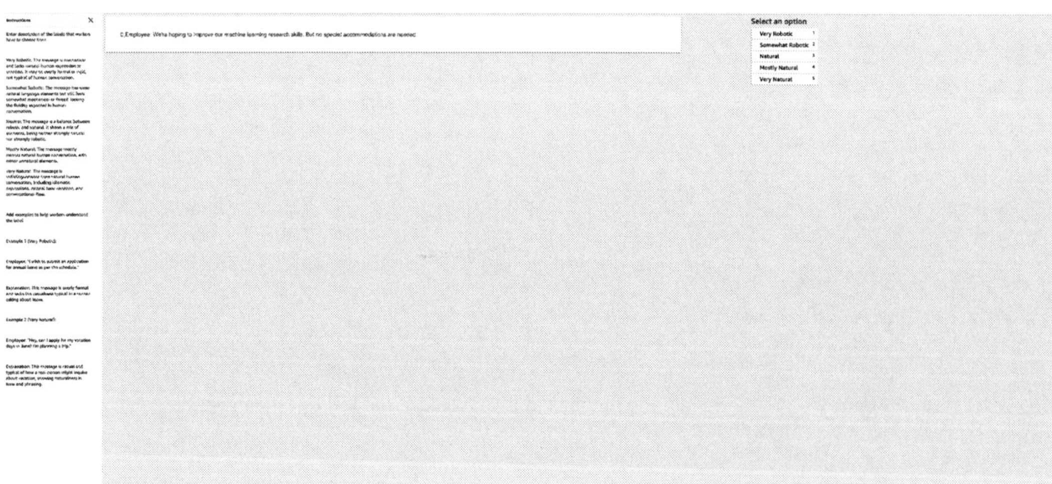

Figure 9: MTurk human instructions to understand if the employee answer is natural

Domain	Number of dialogues
benefits_enrollment	71
performance_review	64
training_request	57
safety_incident_report	103
relocation_request	57
harassment_report	103
goal_setting	42
access_request	278
it_issue_report	38
time_off_report	71

Table 6: HR Multiwoz dataset.

One Example of Generated Dialogues
HR Assistant: Hi there, how can I help you out today? *Employee*: I'm hoping you can help me set up some machine learning training for my team. *HR Assistant*: No problem, tell me a bit about what kind of training you're looking for. What will you guys be learning about and do you need any special accommodations? *Employee*: We're hoping to improve our machine learning research skills. But no special accommodations are needed. *HR Assistant*: Great, how many people will be attending this training? And approximately how long do you think it should last? *Employee*: Three people will be participating and we'd like it to run for two days. *HR Assistant*: Okay, thanks. Do you have a budget in mind for this? It would also help to know what your goals are for your team after the training. *Employee*: Our budget is $5000. We want to come away with better research skills. *HR Assistant*: No problem, when works best for your schedule? Also, do you have a preference for how the training is delivered, like online or in-person? *Employee*: We're hoping for some online seminars on June 15th, 2023. *HR Assistant*: Sounds good. One last thing - would you say your team's current skill level is beginner, intermediate or advanced? And can you provide the contact info for the person coordinating it all? *Employee*: Their level is intermediate. The coordinator is Henry Kim and you can reach him at hkim@researchlab.com or 555-1234.

Table 7: Example of Generated Dialogues

Big City Bias: Evaluating the Impact of Metropolitan Size on Computational Job Market Abilities of Language Models

Charlie Campanella
Indeed
ccampanella@indeed.com

Rob van der Goot
IT University of Copenhagen
robv@itu.dk

Abstract

Large language models (LLMs) have emerged as a useful technology for job matching, for both candidates and employers. Job matching is often based on a particular geographic location, such as a city or region. However, LLMs have known biases, commonly derived from their training data. In this work, we aim to quantify the metropolitan size bias encoded within large language models, evaluating zero-shot salary, employer presence, and commute duration predictions in 384 of the United States' metropolitan regions. Across all benchmarks, we observe negative correlations between the metropolitan size and the performance of the LLMS, indicating that smaller regions are indeed underrepresented. More concretely, the smallest 10 metropolitan regions show upwards of 300% worse benchmark performance than the largest 10.[1]

1 Introduction

Recent large language models (LLMs) are primarily trained on internet-derived corpora (Brown et al., 2020; Touvron et al., 2023a). These underlying datasets are prone to linguistic and geographic bias. For example, the training data of Common Crawl, used to train OpenAI's GPT-3 (Brown et al., 2020) and Meta AI's Llama (Touvron et al., 2023a), is composed of 46% English language documents. Such lexical imbalances contribute to an anglophone bias in various tasks, exemplified by GPT-3.5's "English-first" approach when translating Irish/Gaeilge (Chiarain et al., 2023) and its inability to pass Indonesian primary school exams (Koto et al., 2023) while simultaneously passing U.S. college-entry exams (OpenAI et al., 2023). Evidently, under-representation in training corpora can adversely affect language model performance across various tasks and contexts.

A significant population disparity exists among metropolitan regions in the United States, with the largest, New York–Newark–Jersey City, NY-NJ, having over 300 times more residents than the smallest, Eagle Pass, TX. These population disparities seem to correlate with the amount of associated information available online. For instance, querying "New York, NY" on Wikipedia yields 114,067 results while a search for "Eagle Pass, TX" only returns 1,516 results. The same queries on Google result in 1.7 billion and 8.2 million results, respectively. This training data disparity prompts us to consider whether language models exhibit comparable biases in performance, excelling in tasks associated with larger metropolitan regions.

In this work, we quantify the "big city bias" by evaluating salary, employer presence, and commute duration predictions in the 384 metropolitan statistical areas (MSAs) defined by the United States Census Bureau. Across all benchmarks, analysis indicates a correlation between MSA population and predictive accuracy, indicating superior language model efficacy in the context of larger cities. Given the concentration of technical talent in the United States' 10 most populous metropolitan areas [2], these findings might inspire AI practitioners to look beyond so-called "tech hubs" when applying LLM-generated synthetic data to geographically diverse job matching applications.

We contribute:

- A dataset with population, employer presence, and commute duration for 384 metropolitan areas in the USA.
- Outputs of 5 recent language models predicting employer presence, commute duration, and salary.
- An analysis of the results of the language models for this data and task, showing that larger

[1] https://github.com/charlie-campanella/big-city-bias

[2] https://www.bls.gov/oes/current/oes151252.htm

Proceedings of the First Workshop on Natural Language Processing for Human Resources (NLP4HR 2024), pages 73–77
March 22, 2024

metropolitan areas are more closely associated with accurate predictive outcomes.

2 Methodology

2.1 Data and tasks

Job matching systems are designed to find the best-fitting role for a given candidate. For example, Indeed.com, the world's most popular job site [3], considers a role to be a "bad fit" if there is a salary or geographic mismatch, [4] among other criterion. Our geographically-focused evaluation prompts language models to make *salary*, *employer presence*, and *commute duration* predictions for each metropolitan region to evaluate their performance at common matching tasks.

Prediction biases can reduce the effectiveness of LLM-powered job matching systems. For example, a system which fails to predict salaries within a given region may match job seekers with financially incompatible roles. Inaccurate commute duration forecasts can lead job seekers to consider positions that are logistically unfeasible. Furthermore, not discerning whether an employer's regional presence is a major facility or a branch office can mislead job seekers about career progression prospects.

As mentioned in Section 1, this analysis is conducted on metropolitan areas as defined by the United States Census Bureau. For each task, we leverage data collected from a reputable source, with distributions for each target variable plotted in Figure 1. The data for each task is described in detail below.

Salary Task Data: Sourced from a confidential and proprietary dataset by Indeed.com which includes pre-tax, base annual salaries for registered nurses, software engineers, and warehouse workers in each MSA.

Employer Presence Task Data: Based on a publicly accessible dataset published by People Data Labs [5] which presents the top 10 employers and their respective employment counts across 384 U.S. metropolitan regions. Our modified version of this dataset incorporates additional "state_code" and "metro_state_code" columns, aligning with MSA

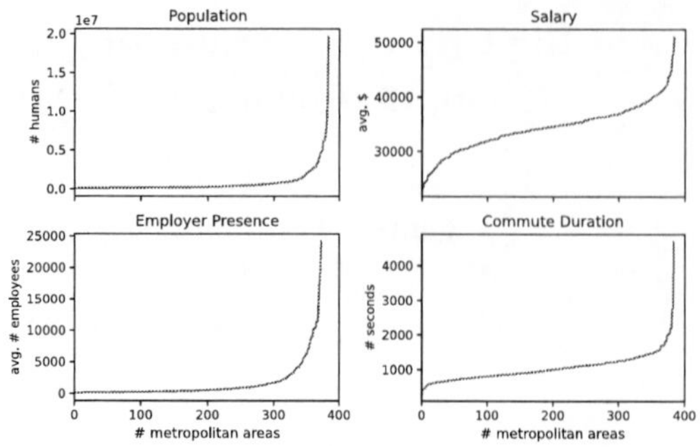

Figure 1: For each variable the cumulative number of metropolitan areas which match a certain threshold (y-axis). Note that the target variables (all except population) are an average over multiple instances within the region, and are thus not directly comparable (i.e. they could be over different sets of jobs, employers, or commutes).

naming conventions used by the U.S. Census Bureau for standardized referencing.

Commute Duration Task Data: Derived from a custom script which uses the Google Maps API to generate 5 random commute origins, destinations, and durations within 20km of the geographic center for each MSA. Note that each duration estimate assumes driving as the mode of transport.

We plot the correlation of the population size and each of the target variables against each other in Figure 2. From this, we can clearly see that the average employer presence and MSA population have a very strong correlation; this makes intuitive sense, as there is greater possibility in larger cities to have larger employers. Other combinations of variables, especially salary and commute duration, show less significant correlation, although the slopes in Figure 1 have similar shapes.

2.2 Models

Our selection of language models was optimized for diversity in architectures, training methods, and parameter size while minimizing computational costs. Based on these criterion, we selected *mistral-instruct-7b-v0.1* (Jiang et al., 2023), *llama-2-chat-7b*, *llama-2-chat-70b* (Touvron et al., 2023b), *gpt-3.5-turbo* (Brown et al., 2020), and *gpt-4* (OpenAI et al., 2023).

We employ these models using prompting, designing task-specific prompts which contain: the question, relevant entities for the task, and instructions on how to structure the answer, so that the numerical response can be automatically extracted.

[3] https://www.indeed.com/about

[4] https://engineering.indeedblog.com/blog/2019/09/jobs-filter/

[5] https://www.peopledatalabs.com/top-employers-dataset

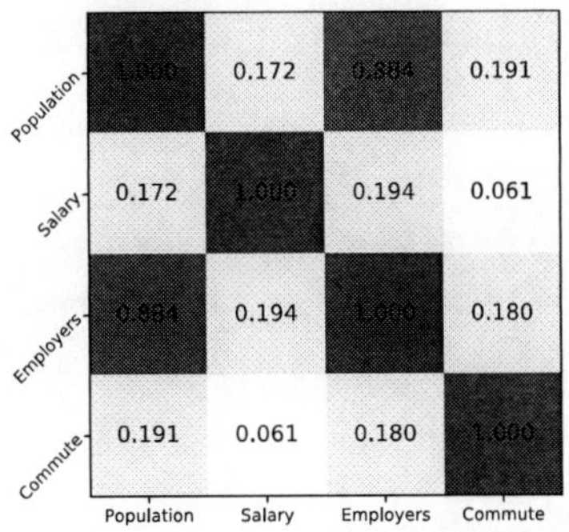

Figure 2: Pearson correlations between MSA population and each target variable. Note that the bottom-left and top-right are mirrored as Pearson correlations are not directional.

All prompts are shown below:

Prompt 2.1: Salary Predictions

> What is the average annual salary for a {JOB_TITLE} in {METRO_AREA}? Return one estimate with no other text, do not return a range. Salary:

Prompt 2.2: Employer Presence Predictions

> How many people does {EMPLOYER_NAME} employ in {METRO_AREA}? Provide an estimate even if this information is not publicly available. Return one estimate with no other text, do not return a range. Number employed:

Prompt 2.3: Commute Duration Predictions

> What is the average driving commute time from {ORIGIN} to {DESTINATION} in {METRO_AREA}? Provide an estimate even though you are not a GPS. Return an estimate in minutes with no other text. Commute Estimate:

2.3 Metrics

After obtaining a response from the language models (Section 2.2), we first extract numerical values through the application of a regular expression (`[^0-9\.]+$`). We compare these numeric values to the gold labels (Section 2.1), and then compute the percentage error for each task. For each task category in a metropolitan region, we take into account 3-5 model outputs and derive an average percentage error. This smooths out individual output variances, ensuring a more reliable evaluation.

Next, we look at the *Pearson correlation* (Pearson, 1901) between the log of the population size and the average prediction error. This will tell us whether larger metropolitan areas consistently have more accurate predictions or vice versa. We then employ the *median error*, as a quantitative metric of the performance of the models. Since this is taken over the values of the variables we predict, and they vary across tasks (Section 2.1), we use our third metric: *coefficient of determination (r^2)*. This metric explains the proportion of the variation in the error that is predictable from the metropolitan size, and normally ranges from 0-1.

LLM	Size	Correl.	Median Err.%	r^2
Salary				
mistral-instruct	7b	-.0890*	21.95	.0079
llama-2-chat	7b	-.3553*	22.92	.1262
llama-2-chat	70b	-.2765*	19.47	.0765
gpt-3.5-turbo	20b	-.3398*	19.49	.1155
gpt-4	?	-.4113*	17.75	.1692
Employer Presence				
mistral-instruct	7b	-.2125*	182.60	.0452
llama-2-chat	7b	-.3307*	201.56	.1094
llama-2-chat	70b	-.2731*	149.36	.0746
gpt-3.5-turbo	20b	-.3004*	161.33	.0902
gpt-4	?	-.3179*	143.45	.1010
Commute Duration				
mistral-instruct	7b	-.1422*	140.22	.0202
llama-2-chat	7b	-.1141*	141.12	.0130
llama-2-chat	70b	-.1915*	126.86	.0367
gpt-3.5-turbo	20b	-.0083*	71.11	.0001
gpt-4	?	-.1872*	51.72	.0351

Table 1: Pearson correlations between the log of the population and the average prediction error, median error, and coefficient of determination (r^2). * $p < 0.0001$.

3 Results

Experimental results are displayed in Table 1. Nearly all experiments demonstrate negative and significant Pearson coefficients, indicating that LLMs tend to achieve better performance in tasks related to larger cities. Commute duration tasks

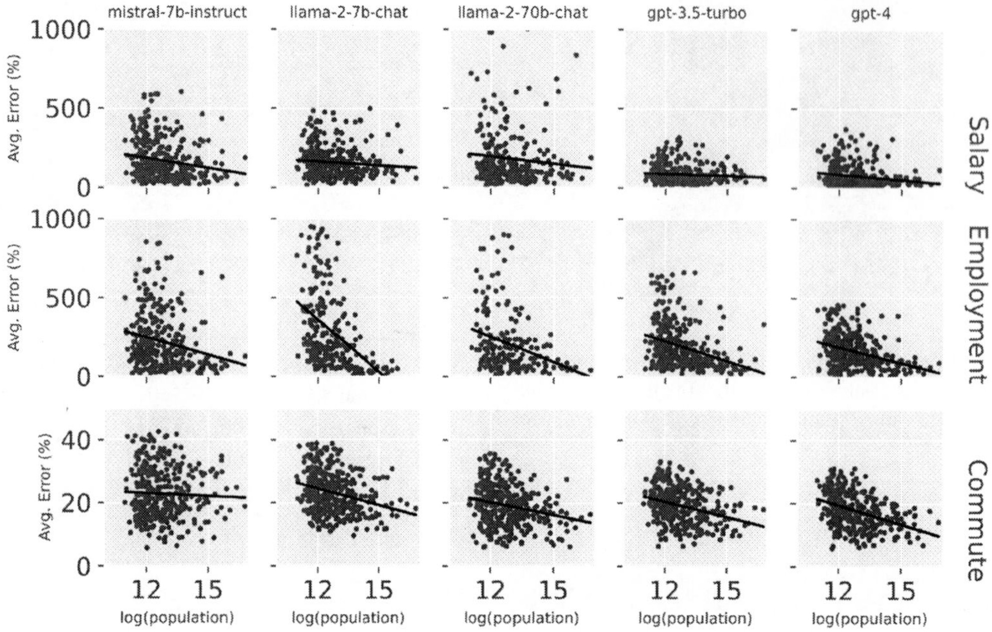

Figure 3: The average error plotted against the log of the population for each task (shown on the right) and each language model (top).

generally show less stable outcomes, with lower correlations and a broader range of median errors, whereas salary prediction tasks consistently present higher correlations and smaller median errors. Median errors are highest for employer presence predictions, which possibly relates to its distribution being the most skewed (Figure 1).

4 Analysis

4.1 Visualizations

Rendering scatterplots of our predictions (Figure 3), we observe the same trend as in Table 1: all correlations are negative to some extent. In these visualizations, we observe that the LLaMA series of language models have the most outliers, with the 70b parameter variant having the most trouble with larger populations (especially for salary). This suggests that larger model size does not necessarily lead to more consistent predictions.

4.2 Top 10 vs Bottom 10

In Table 2, we compare the performance of the language models on the largest and smallest 10 metropolitan areas. It is evident that performance is better for tasks associated with larger regions. While target variable error magnitudes vary greatly, even the approx. 50% average difference among salary tasks is quite noticeable. Performance disparities among commute duration and employer presence are much larger, with up to 9x worse employer presence performance in the bottom 10 metropolitan areas by LLAMA-2-CHAT-7B.

5 Related Work

Research using the open-source PopQA dataset shows that LLMs exhibit worse performance at tasks associated with "popular" entities. (Mallen et al., 2023) Additionally, a separate study reveals a correlation between a nation's GDP-per-capita and performance on related LLM tasks. (Kaplunovich, 2023) While both studies emphasize disparities in LLM task performance based on popularity and/or geography, neither assesses HR-related task performance across metropolitan areas.

6 Conclusion

Large language models, while powerful, show sub-optimal performance in predicting salaries, commute duration, and employer presence in specific regions, with this trend worsening in smaller areas. While LLMs seem unsuitable at generating such job matching data, practitioners should remain vigilant in mitigating geographic bias as these models undergo further development and improvement.

LLM	Size	Top10 Err.%	Bottom10 Err. %	Diff.%
Salary				
mistral-instruct	7b	23.4	25.2	7.6
llama-2-chat	7b	17.4	27.2	56.2
llama-2-chat	70b	14.2	20.1	41.9
gpt-3.5-turbo	20b	15.0	23.3	55.0
gpt-4	?	13.2	23.4	77.0
Employer Presence				
mistral-instruct	7b	240.7	330.7	37.4
llama-2-chat	7b	46.4	467.6	906.9
llama-2-chat	70b	169.5	631.9	272.8
gpt-3.5-turbo	20b	100.1	323.0	222.9
gpt-4	?	68.6	244.2	256.0
Commute Duration				
mistral-instruct	7b	215.0	431.7	100.8
llama-2-chat	7b	155.7	268.9	72.7
llama-2-chat	70b	169.5	631.9	272.8
gpt-3.5-turbo	20b	83.4	188.5	125.9
gpt-4	?	56.5	232.8	312.4

Table 2: Performance of language models on the 10 largest and 10 smallest metropolitan areas. The "Diff.%" column indicates the normalized percentage increase in error when comparing the bottom 10 to the top 10. i.e. a diff/% of 10 means that the error is 10% higher for the bottom 10 as compared to the top 10.

Limitations

Our study's primary limitation lies in the inherent nature of language models as probabilistic systems, which leads to inconsistent outputs. For example, generating LLAMA-2-CHAT-7B employment presence predictions only yielded 259 valid, non-outlier data points, less than other models. Additionally, our research was predominantly U.S.-centric, limiting its applicability to other geographical contexts. Another limitation is our focus on absolute error metrics, which fail to indicate whether the model systematically overestimates or underestimates certain variables, like salaries. Addressing these issues in future research could improve accuracy and applicability.

References

Tom Brown, Benjamin Mann, Nick Ryder, Melanie Subbiah, Jared D Kaplan, Prafulla Dhariwal, Arvind Neelakantan, Pranav Shyam, Girish Sastry, Amanda Askell, et al. 2020. Language models are few-shot learners. *Advances in neural information processing systems*, 33:1877–1901.

Neasa-Ni Chiarain, Oisín Nolan, Neimhin-Robinson Gunning, and Madeleine Comtois. 2023. Filling the slate: examining the contribution llms can make in irish story content generation. In *Proc. 9th Workshop on Speech and Language Technology in Education (SLaTE)*, pages 176–181.

Albert Q Jiang, Alexandre Sablayrolles, Arthur Mensch, Chris Bamford, Devendra Singh Chaplot, Diego de las Casas, Florian Bressand, Gianna Lengyel, Guillaume Lample, Lucile Saulnier, et al. 2023. Mistral 7b. *arXiv preprint arXiv:2310.06825*.

A. Kaplunovich. 2023. Wealth of nations, wealth of data: How gdp shapes diverse large language models like chatgpt : Interviewing assorted open source generative ai models. In *2023 IEEE International Conference on Big Data (BigData)*, pages 4654–4663, Los Alamitos, CA, USA. IEEE Computer Society.

Fajri Koto, Nurul Aisyah, Haonan Li, and Timothy Baldwin. 2023. Large language models only pass primary school exams in Indonesia: A comprehensive test on IndoMMLU. In *Proceedings of the 2023 Conference on Empirical Methods in Natural Language Processing*, pages 12359–12374, Singapore. Association for Computational Linguistics.

Alex Mallen, Akari Asai, Victor Zhong, Rajarshi Das, Daniel Khashabi, and Hannaneh Hajishirzi. 2023. When not to trust language models: Investigating effectiveness of parametric and non-parametric memories. In *Proceedings of the 61st Annual Meeting of the Association for Computational Linguistics (Volume 1: Long Papers)*, pages 9802–9822, Toronto, Canada. Association for Computational Linguistics.

OpenAI, J. Achiam, S. Adler, S. Agarwal, L. Ahmad, I. Akkaya, F. L. Aleman, D. Almeida, J. Altenschmidt, S. Altman, S. Anadkat, R. Avila, I. Babuschkin, S. Balaji, V. Balcom, P. Baltescu, H. Bao, M. Bavarian, and B. Belgum, J. ... Zoph. 2023. Gpt-4 technical report.

Karl Pearson. 1901. LIII. on lines and planes of closest fit to systems of points in space. *The London, Edinburgh, and Dublin Philosophical Magazine and Journal of Science*, 2(11):559–572.

Hugo Touvron, Thibaut Lavril, Gautier Izacard, Xavier Martinet, Marie-Anne Lachaux, Timothée Lacroix, Baptiste Rozière, Naman Goyal, Eric Hambro, Faisal Azhar, et al. 2023a. Llama: Open and efficient foundation language models. *arXiv preprint arXiv:2302.13971*.

Hugo Touvron, Louis Martin, Kevin Stone, Peter Albert, Amjad Almahairi, Yasmine Babaei, Nikolay Bashlykov, Soumya Batra, Prajjwal Bhargava, Shruti Bhosale, et al. 2023b. Llama 2: Open foundation and fine-tuned chat models. *arXiv preprint arXiv:2307.09288*.

Author Index

Association for Computational Linguistics
209 N. Eighth Street
Stroudsburg, Pennsylvania 18360

CURRAN ASSOCIATES INC.
proceedings.com

ISBN 978-1-7138-9457-5

9 781713 894575

9th Workshop on Slavic Natural Language Processing (SlavicNLP 2023)

Dubrovnik, Croatia
6 May 2023